Master Media Relations

The Complete Guide To Getting Better Press Coverage

Donna Giancontieri

iUniverse, Inc.
New York   Bloomington

Master Media Relations

The Complete Guide To Getting Better Press Coverage

iUniverse books may be ordered through booksellers or by contacting:

iUniverse
1663 Liberty Drive
Bloomington, IN 47403
www.iuniverse.com
1-800-Authors (1-800-288-4677)

ISBN: 978-1-4401-0903-4 (pbk)
ISBN: 978-1-4401-0904-1 (ebk)

Edited by Joseph P. Shaw

Printed in the United States of America

iUniverse rev. date: 11/20/2008

Master Media Relations

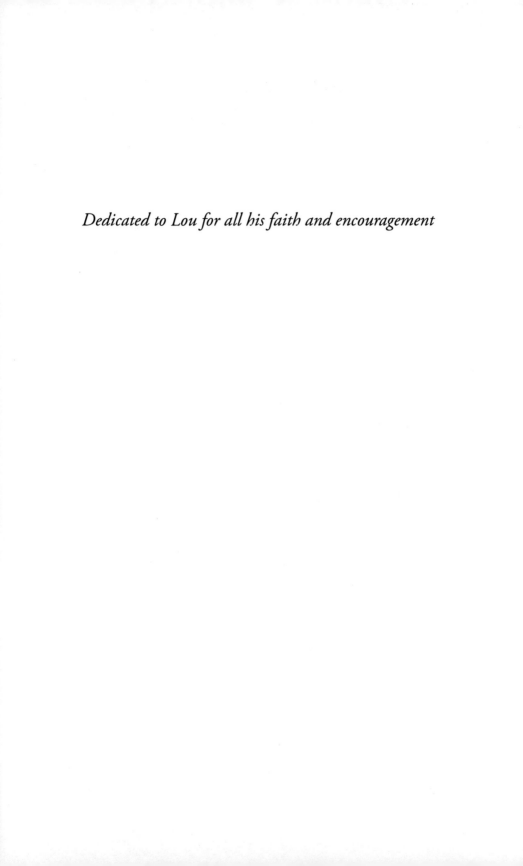

Dedicated to Lou for all his faith and encouragement

Contents

Introduction

There is a connotation with the term "source" that conjures up an image of a clandestine meeting, a "Deepthroat" giving away secrets, or an anonymous caller. But in reality, a news source is anyone who provides information to a reporter. If you deal with the media as part of your job or if you speak to reporters to promote your business, campaign, or cause, then you are a news source.

Master Media Relations is a strategic plan to help professionals navigate the unchartered territories of press coverage. Why must every spokesperson, public official, and business owner read this book? Because it covers every base, includes pointers for any news source in any circumstance.

Effectively reacting to the media is more important than ever before. The dynamics of technology allow every quote, every photo, every editorial, and every misstep to be forever accessed online. A story produced in Dallas can be almost instantly spread to Manhattan and London and Hong Kong. News spreads fast these days. Stories are posted on web sites within minutes, deadlines are much shorter, and sources must respond rapidly and accurately.

Facing a news reporter can be intimidating for anyone. Even articulate attorneys, verbose politicians, and stoic law enforcement agents can be rendered speechless by the knowledge that what they are about to say will appear in print or on television or radio. An unprepared and antsy news source can cause damage to their company, their reputation, or their business.

But if you are prepared, dealing with reporters can be a productive and even enjoyable experience.

A few examples:

- The accomplishments of a newly formed crime unit in a small police department gained sudden media attention. The sergeant found himself the reluctant spokesperson. A seasoned law enforcement agent, he nonetheless provided more information to the reporter than he intended, potentially comprising an investigation. None of his staff knew how to write a press release or how to handle such intense and unexpected media attention. By reading *Master Media Relations,* he would have been prepared beforehand.

- A real estate agent received calls from reporters seeking comment about the increased competition to close deals. Indeed, the unstable economy had created a ruthless atmosphere she had not previously witnessed in her business. Should she agree to the interview? She didn't want to bash her industry but she might benefit professionally from having her name published. How could she be honest without sounding negative and critical?

- A dedicated parent ran for a seat on the local school board. She faced a campaign and, if successful, monthly board meetings covered by the press. The school board manages an annual budget that comprises 50% of each resident's property tax bill, a contentious issue and a hot news topic. She needed comprehensive advice on how to be prepared for this new role.

- A non-profit sought media attention with the hope of generating donations. Press releases describing their programs failed to produce coverage. The administrator was advised to invite a reporter to spend several days observing one of the group's programs. The community newspaper printed several articles plus numerous photos. Larger publications picked up the story and the non-profit received a barrage of donations.

The first step toward polishing skills as a news source is to develop a keen understanding of how the media works. Once you learn to grasp the fundamentals of what editors and reporters need, you instantly gain a competitive edge.

Foremost, it is essential to understand that news is a business. Remember William Randolph Hearst's infamous fabrications aimed at selling more newspapers? Generating revenue is one of a publisher's main goals. Of course, Hearst's extreme mix of journalism and sensationalism was an anomaly. The majority of media outlets are sincerely trying to provide accurate and fair coverage. Still, keeping in mind that news is a business is essential for all savvy news sources.

The Business of News

Do reporters see themselves as watchdogs? Of course. As the Fourth Estate? Maybe. Do many reporters at some point in their careers aspire to be the next Woodward or Bernstein? Probably.

Indeed, we may have an image of the crusty editor working in a dim office, sleeves rolled, tie loosened, surrounded by busy reporters in cubicles pounding away on keyboards, phone to their ear, trying to meet a deadline. Some version of this depiction probably holds true in most newsrooms.

But remember, in the larger office up the hall from all this commotion sits the publisher counting the company's receivables. Media outlets make money by selling a variety of news and information just as supermarkets generate income by selling a variety of groceries. The wider the array of compelling news, the larger the audience. And, of course, a larger audience means more paid advertisements. Standard business practice.

You may recall when *Time* magazine labeled the summer of 2001 as "The Summer of The Shark." During a season of otherwise lackluster news, a media frenzy surrounded a string of shark attacks. Images of bloody victims and menacing sharks appeared on the front pages of newspapers and magazines nationwide and topped television news broadcasts.

In fact, there were fewer shark attacks in 2001 than in previous years (this bit of statistical information was mentioned in some stories, typically in passing at the end) but that particular summer the incidents occurred within a condensed time frame and at popular beaches. The blast of reports captured interest. News of every attack, every shark spotted within a few hundred yards of any beach, tapped deeper into our natural fascination and fear of the predators. Publishers sold more newspapers: television news ratings soared. The shark attacks sold news.

A good media outlet delivers stories that resonate with a wide audience. Abstract doesn't sell. Stories that sell will educate, inform, tap into a concern or fear, or promise to solve a problem. Sources should always keep that in mind when pitching story ideas to reporters.

A News Source

While publishers are overseeing the financial aspect of the news business, reporters and editors are scrambling to the finish line with the story. They need accurate, interesting news that will draw a larger audience than rival newspapers, magazines, Internet sites, or television and radio stations. A reporter wants the story first, and they want the facts fast. And to accomplish this, they need sources.

News is game of mutual support. A news outlet with a reputation for providing accurate, fair, and interesting coverage is the best place for any spokesperson in any circumstance to convey a message. And to gain that reputable image, news outlets rely on a diverse and knowledgeable group of reliable sources. *A spokesperson's level of skill has a considerable impact on the resulting news piece.*

For the past decade, the news industry has undergone a major transition. Print newspapers are fading fast—circulation is down and advertising revenue is plummeting. Meanwhile, media consumption is growing on the Internet. Even small circulation papers have their own web sites. Breaking news alerts flash simultaneously on computers and Blackberries worldwide. Some news is considered stale by the time the next edition of a daily newspaper hits the stands. The digital age has changed the face of the traditional media.

Still, it is likely that the impact of the digital age on community newspapers over the next decade will be somewhat less intensive. In many smaller communities, folks still want to pick up their local paper and read the news the traditional way. News in small towns is more focused, more detailed, and sources must be even more prepared before agreeing to interviews with reporters.

But no matter what type of news outlet you are dealing with (newspapers, online news sites, radio, television) getting the word out means hitting all the bases. It is no longer enough just to send out a simple press release and hope you land on the front page. The digital age requires more of you as a news source.

By understanding how the media works, a news source can effectively polish an image, deflect bad coverage, educate the public, and promote an agenda.

Whether you are trying to promote your business, your cause, or your campaign—or even if you are firmly planted in the hot seat answering tricky questions—the tips presented in this book will prepare you for what to expect when dealing with reporters, help you to establish yourself as a credible news source, and guide you toward better press coverage.

Step One:
Interview Clinic

A former colleague of mine found himself in a position where he was required, for the first time, to participate in frequent media interviews. He started off a bit shaky but eventually became an accomplished spokesperson—knowledgeable, able to shed some positive influence on the coverage, and, for the most part, able to stay off the hot seat.

When I asked him what he had learned about interacting with reporters during the six years he held that post, he summed it up succinctly: "I learned not to say anything that will come back to bite me in the behind."

Celebrities, CEOs and politicians have access to professional publicists for guidance. Publicists help them prepare for interviews, polish their image, and promote themselves, their business, their campaign, or their cause. But the majority of news sources don't have this luxury and can have some difficulty getting good press coverage—or getting any coverage at all.

A seasoned law enforcement officer told me he "throws up his hands" whenever a reporter calls—he simply does not know how to handle the questions. An administrator at a non-profit complained that she just didn't know how to get her organization's programs into the local newspaper. A garrulous elected official often revealed details he did not intend to provide to reporters.

Most news sources learn about media relations, just as my colleague did, by trial and error—or trial by fire.

Good press coverage starts with the basics of the interview. How you approach the discussion, whether it is on the phone, in person or on camera, sets the tone for the entire news piece.

Being interviewed can be intimidating, but once you are comfortable with these types of discussions, you will begin to view them as opportunities for promotion, and you might even begin to enjoy them.

The trick, again, in the simplest terms used by my former colleague, is mostly to just avoid saying or doing anything that will come back to bite you. And there are steps you can take to make sure you say exactly what you mean, and to position yourself within the news to your best advantage.

Getting Your Message Across

Each news story is built in steps around a central topic and using a specific architectural framework. Spokespersons can gain an advantage if they prepare notes and provide input using the same structure that journalists use to fashion their stories.

Although there are numerous strategies now deployed in journalism, most simple news stories are constructed using what is called the "inverted pyramid." It is precisely what it sounds like—an upside-down pyramid: The vital information is placed at the beginning of the story, with details diminishing in importance as the story progresses. Ideally, the essence of the story should be immediately revealed. Stories are constructed this way for a reason: The core issue will be still be conveyed even if the second half is cut by an editor or producer because of space or time constraints, or if the reader moves on after just a few paragraphs. (It first became part of journalism in the 19th century for a more utilitarian reason: The articles were being transmitted by telegraph wire, and the system was terribly unreliable. So sending the most important information first was a way of making sure it had the best chance of getting through.)

Understanding the inverted pyramid theory will help you prioritize your talking points to ensure that the most important elements get prominent play in the news piece.

In a standard news story, the central questions—Who? What? Where? When? and Why?—are answered very early in the story. The bulk of this information is provided in the lede, the article's first paragraph. (This is also sometimes spelled *lead*, depending on the journalist's preference.)

Two or three paragraphs following the lede often contain a quote and usually include what is referred to as the "nut graph," a paragraph summarizing the point of the article "in a nutshell," offering a brief summary of facts to swiftly educate the reader on the topic and to explain why the story is important. The angle of the story becomes clear within these first paragraphs. Background, supporting information and colorful details are peppered throughout the remainder of the piece.

Any reporter will tell you that at some point in his or her career an editor has scolded, "Don't bury the lede!" *The essential information must be at the top of the story.* If the pertinent facts are buried, the real news gets lost and the peripheral information takes over. It also helps capture attention quickly.

Apply this same advice to every interaction you have with the media. When preparing notes for an interview, a press release, a speech, or even a letter to the editor, the inverted pyramid rule should be followed. Position the most important information first, and then incrementally scale down to the fluff.

Your written talking points likewise should be listed in order of importance. The first three are your main message points. These should be repeated and re-enforced several times during interviews.

A news story is a snapshot, a thumbnail sketch of a larger picture. Space and time constraints dictate how much of the story a media outlet can report. You spent months working on a project, but now a reporter has just a few hours to learn about it, interview sources, and write the story (along with several other articles, typically) by deadline. Radio and television reporters can have as little as 30 seconds for a report on a complicated issue. Make the information you provide count.

When dealing with the media, always temper your expectations, and always stay focused on the most important message points. If the reporter needs more information, you can provide the subtext and ancillary details later. Initially, stick to the core message. The main points of any story can easily get lost if the reporter is given a bounty of excess information.

Tip: When you drift outside your main message, even briefly, you risk swaying the story. A simple phrase can bounce you off course, or even into the hot seat.

Every word you say counts, especially if you have a competitor or adversary. News is very concise. The most interesting comments and the most colorful stories get play. By carefully preparing your comments and staying focused on main message points, you won't risk accidentally saying or doing something that creates conflict and results in a story angle you did not expect.

Don't hand the media or your adversaries something to exploit. Never use a negative theme or topic as an analogy or comparison. Keep the discussion positive.

Be careful about casually tossing around volatile words. Excusing yourself from a presentation because of an "emergency" meeting can drum up all sorts of negative press and speculation. Do you actually just have a scheduling conflict? Then say so. Don't excuse yourself from one obligation by making the other commitment sound more important with an explanation of an "urgent" or "emergency" meeting. You may end up fielding questions about the "emergency" when in fact there isn't one.

Reporters are often accused of not telling the "whole story." And this is true—they don't, because they can't possibly report every fact and every quote they gather. They must decide how to build the story by selecting which components will be included and which will be left out. These decisions are often made quickly, under deadline.

So, make it easier for them, and safer for you: provide the pertinent facts in order of importance. By taking time to organize your comments under the same inverted pyramid structure that journalists use, you have a better chance of landing an advantageous spot within the story.

Consider This: One Phrase Can Sway the Angle of the Story

In early 2008, Michelle Obama was campaigning for her husband, Barack Obama. At a rally in Wisconsin, she discussed the details of her husband's agenda, working hard to bolster his image and promote his presidential campaign. But her message became clouded in controversy over a single comment among many she made that day.

Fourteen words changed a positive story into a negative one:

"For the first time in my adult life, I am proud of my country," Mrs. Obama told a crowd of supporters.

Her husband's adversaries pounced. First time she has been proud? How anti-American! How utterly unpatriotic! The comment aired on news broadcasts nationwide and was played and replayed on the Internet, obscuring the broader message she tried to convey that day.

Positioning Yourself Within the Story

To sell newspapers or attract viewers, media outlets must deliver compelling stories. Good stories capture the 3 C's: conflict, change and color. The foundation of any interesting news story must have these three elements. Conflict and change, in particular, translate into a news hook, a captivating component aimed at drawing the interest of the audience.

Without the 3 C's, news is repetitive and boring. Reporters must capitalize on the nuances, the elements of any story that spice it up and capture an audience's attention.

Rate the following stories on a scale from 1 to 10. Are they newsworthy? Would you read the article if this was the headline?

- Police arrest man for drug possession

- Construction begins on a new subdivision

- Local restaurant closes

- A new diet book is published

- The new school year kicks off

- Candidates announced in upcoming election

They rate about a 3 on my scale. But add the news hooks, and they become stories that will grab an audience's attention:

- High school teacher arrested for drug possession

- New housing development blocks water views of 20 neighbors

- Popular restaurant owners retire after 40 years in same location

- New diet promises miraculous results by eating chocolate

- Kindergarten enrollment highest ever at local schools

- Retired minister announces mayoral run against longtime incumbent

These stories contain conflict and change. Add some color—quotes, descriptions, images—and we have fully fleshed-out news items.

A drug arrest *is* newsworthy. But when the defendant is a teacher arrested at the school, it becomes a front-page story.

More new houses? Ho-hum. But if officials approved zoning relief allowing the addition of a third story that blocks the neighbors' view, then there is conflict.

A new school year starting? Happens every year. However, cute pictures of fidgety students on their first day in jam-packed classrooms could make the front page.

News is a competitive business. Editors sift through ideas and choose the most appealing stories. A journalist's philosophy for selecting newsworthy stories is relatively simple: He or she considers the basic story idea, looks for a news hook, and then applies the "so what?" test.

- Kindergarten enrollment is high. *So what?* Classrooms are overcrowded.

- A new diet book came out. *So what?* It advocates eating chocolate to lose weight.

Before pitching an idea to a journalist or agreeing to an interview, make sure you apply your own "so what?" test. Find your optimal position within the news and steer the interview in that direction.

For example, your business is having a sale. *So what?* It is not a story. It is an ad. Try this: Your business is having a sale. *So what?* Half the proceeds will be donated to a local family with an ill child. That version of the story is newsworthy.

Within the overall topic of every news story is the angle. The angle slants the story in one direction or the other, providing the tone.

The story of the popular teacher arrested for drug possession has many potential angles. One reporter might slant the story toward the concerned parents who are worried that students might have had access to the drugs. Another reporter might highlight criticism of the police for making the arrest in front of students. A third might focus on the drug prevention classes added to the school's curriculum as a result of the arrest.

There are many reasons a reporter will slant a story one way or the other. *Initial reaction from sources is often a key turning point.*

An astute news source presents a story with a fresh angle using the same philosophy journalists' use. When looking at a potential news story, positive or negative, ask yourself these questions:

- How is this interesting?

- How will I be positioned in this story?

- How can I shift the direction to my advantage?

- What questions can I expect with regard to the change or conflict?

Keep your expectations for coverage reasonable and find a captivating hook and angle within the broader topic. I have seen countless news sources rage in disappointment because "their" story was overlooked. You can't always change what a reporter chooses to write, or what an editor decides to print or where they place the story. To some extent, you can, however, remain in control, reduce misstatements, and avoid fallout from mistakes. You can maintain a positive spin on your image. (More on publicity strategies later in the book)

Examine angles that enhance your position within the story or improve your chances for coverage. For instance, dovetail your pitch with a growing trend, an upcoming holiday, or a popular event. Offer a solution or promote some type of change. Pull at some heartstrings. One story can have many angles. Find one that benefits you, and then steer the story in that direction.

Consider This: Positioning

A panel of elected officials learned during a crowded public meeting that a property owner installed a concrete barrier on a public path to the beach that is adjacent to his home.

Reporters took notes, likely planning to gather more information following the meeting. Presumably, they would have contacted the person who installed the obstacle, called other neighbors, and taken photos. At some point, the reporters would have contacted one or more of the elected officials seeking reaction.

But in this instance, the angle of the story was upended. Upon learning of the barrier, one of the elected officials leapt to his feet, excused himself from the meeting, invited reporters to accompany him and drove to the beach. Standing in the sand in his business attire, he pounded his fist on the irksome blockade, cited the rights of all beachgoers to access the shoreline and promised action. Within hours, he had arranged for the removal of the obstacle.

The angle of the story instantly shifted toward him—the champion of every constituent who frequented that beach.

This is a dramatic illustration—a true story—and a good example of how a source steered the direction of a story with his initial reaction. By taking a broad look at any given story and deciding how you want to be positioned within the context, it is possible to shift the angle.

Preparing For the Interview

Interviews with the media can happen spontaneously, or they can be pre-arranged. They can be welcome or considered an intrusion. No matter the situation, you should prepare the same way.

First, take a few minutes and organize your thoughts. Prepare talking points, in writing, for reference during the interview. Highlight the top three points you want to come across in the news piece. During the discussion, redirect the conversation back to those three points as often as you can.

Keep your message points brief and direct. Every quote should be concise and clear and should sum up your position. If you call or meet with a reporter without organizing your thoughts, the interview can easily wander into areas you don't expect. Set the course yourself, and stay in control by outlining the salient points.

If you suspect you might need support staff to chime in, call them in before the interview. Interrupting an interview to call in a colleague disrupts the flow of the conversation.

Have reports, agendas or press releases ready to distribute prior to the interview. If time allows, provide the written material in advance of the interview. Every reporter has been in a situation where he or she is attempting to interview a source about a written document without having the opportunity to read it thoroughly. The reporter is forced to get the basic elements and then must play catch-up later after digesting the material. You both end up wasting time with follow-up interviews.

Tip: *Never do an interview when you are tired, angry, or emotional.*

Finally, decide how much time you have to devote to a discussion so you can tell the reporter at the beginning of the interview. Typically, 20 to 30 minutes is adequate for most interviews, unless the subject matter is very comprehensive.

With televised interviews, the reporter will often suggest a pre-interview—if they don't suggest one, you should pitch the idea. This provides you with a better handle on the questions to be asked and gives you a little "rehearsal" time. (More about on-camera interviews later.)

You should never ask a print reporter for a pre-interview, but you can certainly ask them to be specific about the topic of discussion and the angle of the article. Asking them when they suspect that the story will run is perfectly acceptable as well. If you would like a copy, or a copy of a photograph, offer to pay for them.

Before the interview, prepare one "wrap-up" response. Many reporters end an interview by asking "Is there anything else you'd like to add?" Be prepared to do so with a one-sentence, positive comment that sums up your main message. You also may want to use this opportunity to suggest other sources the reporter may benefit from interviewing.

Don't thank the reporter too profusely or express overt gratitude for the interview ... it may backfire on you. Reporters never want to be made to feel as though they are doing a source a favor or acting as a PR flack.

Before pitching a story or agreeing to an interview:

Understand the concept of a news hook.

Apply the "so what?" test.

Gather all the facts so you are educated and prepared.

Consider your position within the story.

Prepare your talking points.

Steer the interview in the direction of your preferred angle.

Off Course? Smooth Transitions Back to Message Points

If the conversation drifts off course, away from your main message points, be sure to reel it back in as quickly as possible. Don't wander into areas that could change the angle of the story and your position within. This can happen when a reporter asks you midstream to respond to an adversary's criticism or an ancillary problem related to the issue. Respond quickly to any questions that appear to be leading the discussion in a different direction, and then veer right back to your message points.

Don't be afraid to ask to have your quotes read back to you—that is perfectly acceptable. But never ask to see the entire story before it goes to print. A reporter has no obligation to show you, and you have no right to ask.

Remember, keep your comments brief and to the point. Long, rambling sentences are difficult for journalists to quote or to paraphrase. And truncated quotes can result in a skewed message.

Five effective phrases to transition back to your main message points:

"As I mentioned ... "

"That is an interesting point, but our main consideration is ... "

"We need to remember that the issue here is ... "

"The important point in all of this is ... "

"I want to make sure everyone understands that ... "

Look for Signs of Confusion

A skilled journalist will ask as many questions as necessary to fill in all the gaps to complete the story. But beware the novice (or tired, distracted or overworked) reporter who may not want to admit he or she isn't sure of all the details.

Look for signs that they are not following the discussion. Pay attention to the line of questions. After you provide an answer to a specific question, there are logical follow-up questions—*if* the reporter understands the concept. If they switch gears or ask questions that don't align with the conversation, guide the discussion back to the beginning and repeat what you have already said. If they continue to take notes, they probably didn't get it the first time around.

Hone your listening skills; make sure that you and the reporter are in sync. Politely correct any mistakes in a reporter's question before you respond to the actual inquiry. This helps both of you—remember, the reporter wants the story to be accurate as much as you do. While simultaneously working on numerous stories, journalists must become instant experts on several topics at once. It's a difficult task. As a news source, it is your obligation to make sure they understand the issue and that they have all the necessary facts and background.

Listen to that inner voice in your head that is telling you when a reporter just doesn't get it. If possible and appropriate, toss in an anecdote or a story of a comparative situation as a way to make the topic clearer.

Pay attention to body language: furrowed brows, glancing back at notes on previous pages while you talk, not making eye contact, a bouncing leg, long hesitations between questions—all can be signs that a reporter isn't following the conversation but may be 1) uncomfortable admitting he or she doesn't understand, or 2) on such a tight deadline that he or she just needs to get the notes down and move on with the intention of re-reading, and grasping, it later.

If the interview concludes and you still are still unsure if the reporter understands, suggest another source to contact as a follow-up. If you have lingering concerns that the story will not accurately portray your position, write a letter to the editor that outlines all you main message points. Submit the letter for publication to run in the same edition as the story. Or contact the television producer and go over your main message points.

Hone Your Listening Skills:

Pay Full Attention. Hold the interview in a quiet setting; don't take phone calls or sort paperwork during the discussion.

Focus on the Question. Repeat the question in your mind before replying to reinforce the exact wording.

Don't interrupt. Let the reporter finish the entire question before responding, correcting him or her, or countering facts within the question. If you begin preparing your reply before he or she has finished speaking, then you haven't *really* heard the question.

Keep your emotions in check. Once you begin blaming, criticizing and judging in your head, you have stopped listening.

Clarify the question with your own question. "When you ask me this ... do you mean ...? Or "It sounds like you are saying ... am I correct with that assumption?"

When to Answer…And When Not to

In the editorial room at the newspaper where I once worked, there was a running joke about a character on the Simpsons who, when faced with a question he really didn't want to answer, replied: "Short answer—yes, with an if. Long answer—no, with a but."

Every reporter at one time or another has dealt with a cagey response like that—the lexicon might be different, but the essence of the non-reply is the same. An answer like that typically results in one of two outcomes: the reporter digs deeper to see why you are being so noncommittal, or they drop you from the story completely and rely on other sources.

Tip: Answer a question honestly and completely, or you shouldn't answer it at all.

There might be times when you just don't want to answer a question—and often you might have valid reasons. Perhaps you don't know the answer, the issue is confidential, or you don't know how to respond without making yourself, or someone else, look bad.

If you don't know the answer, just say so, then promise to find out and provide he reporter with the information prior to deadline. *And follow through—every time.*

Perhaps you can't answer the question because you risk leaking confidential information. Learn what is public information and what is confidential within the context of your position. If you are unsure, check with a boss or an attorney.

Afraid you'll say the wrong thing? Take your time and craft your response. Remember, just because a question has been posed to you doesn't mean you must answer it that minute. Take time to prepare, write down some talking points, gather information. Get the reporter's deadline, prepare yourself, then do the interview. Off-the-cuff replies can get you in trouble, so take your time—even if it is ten minutes—to prepare.

Remember: You never want to be in the position where you have divulged confidential information. Conversely, you never want to be in the position of denying members of the press public information they are entitled to have.

Never comment when asked about something you haven't seen or read yourself. You may be asked to comment on a press release or a report that the reporter has read but that you haven't yet seen. *I repeat: Don't comment until you have read it yourself.* Reporters may offer to read portions and then ask for your comments. It's risky to offer an opinion or a solution when you are not familiar with the subject matter. If you misspeak and then are forced to explain later that you commented without having read the document, you look incompetent and irresponsible. Get a copy yourself—ask the reporter to forward one to you if you can't obtain one quickly. Read it, in its entirety, and then reply to the reporter's questions.

If you are unsure about how to handle a specific media inquiry, don't hesitate to ask your company's lawyers or your personal attorney for some guidance. They will likely guide you to the cautionary side but the advice may be very helpful if the issue is sensitive.

Newspaper articles are often referenced in court proceedings. So be careful with any issue that has a legal angle to it. Get an attorney's advice if necessary. But weigh that advice against your obligation to provide public information or your desire for publicity. Lawyers will take the extreme cautionary tack and often are not considered the best news sources.

Lastly, and most importantly, whenever you are responding to any type of media inquiry, be sure you have *all the facts* before you reply. Educate yourself on the topic. Never wing it. You aren't doing yourself, or the reporter, any favors if you fudge an answer or provide inadequate information.

Don't Know the Answer to a Reporter's Question?

If you don't know the answer to the question, admit it. Never guess, lie or provide a partial response. Again, once you are quoted, it is there forever. Make sure you are accurate with the facts, every time.

Tell the reporter you will find out and call them back. Then do it—before his or her deadline.

Your response should be: "*I am not certain of the answer to that question, and I want to give you the accurate response, so I will double-check and get back to you as soon as I can.*"

The most important part of this type of situation is to follow through with the promise to get the information for them.

When the Facts Are Fluid

Some stories are moving targets. The information you provide during an interview could be outdated by the time the news airs or goes to print.

In these cases, ask the reporter to call you one last time right before deadline to follow up and see if there are any changes. If you don't hear back and there are some new facts, call the newsroom an hour before deadline. If the reporter is not available, ask to speak to an editor or another staff member and provide the information.

Don't allow outdated information to be used by the press with the intention of updating it for the next broadcast or issue. Bad information and old data can lead to all types of misunderstandings and problems.

Ditch the Technical Jargon

I can't stress this enough: Speak as plainly as possible. Even the simplest technical jargon can confuse a reporter, or the audience, and it can skew the story.

Journalists must become instant experts on the topics they write about. Keep in mind that they are not lawyers, accountants, engineers, or doctors. Speak as if you are explaining to a high school student. This is not meant as a disparaging comment toward reporters—it's just a logical strategy that helps them as much as you. You can't expect a member of the press to understand when one source starts talking about "footprints" on site plans, the next source mentions LOSAP in relation to an emergency response story, and still another casually refers to the "stip" in an ongoing legal matter. These terms become part of your everyday lexicon, but they might mean nothing to a journalist.

Never use acronyms unless you are sure the reporter is familiar with them. If you must use them, prepare a written list of any acronyms you use and give them the list prior to the interview.

Speak plainly and provide the general details. A reporter can seek more specific and technical information on the minutia if they need it later.

It's also interesting to note that most newspapers are written at a fifth grade to seventh grade reading level—so remember to keep it simple.

Avoiding Dull Quotes

Okay, let's start with the worst, most over-used quote of all. Use it, and I can pretty much guarantee you won't be quoted if any decent editor has anything to say about it:

"It's a win-win for everybody." That quote is a lose-lose.

Don't utter those six dull words. It's been printed countless times. It's boring. But for some reason, sources tend to use this comment over and over.

Tip: If you want your quote to trump others in the context of any type of news piece, avoid clichéd and overused phrases.

One of the basic rules of writing is to use active verbs—jump, spin, run, twist. If you are hoping to be quoted, come up with an active comment. Or use a clever comparison. But always keep it brief and to the point.

If you want to be quoted, be colorful. Create a fresh angle. Use a catchy comment, or something just slightly different from others interviewed on the same topic, and you will get top billing in the article.

And avoid negative words that might just land you in trouble because they are perceived as condescending or prejudicial. For instance, if you are trying to express that a particular group of people is upset over a specific situation, say members of the group are "frustrated." Never say they are "bitter," which has a negative connotation. Choose your words carefully. Another example: Never say a person or group "clings to" a resource. They "rely on" the resource is a much better option. See the distinction?

Also, avoid absolutes—don't use "always" and "never" unless you are certain beyond a doubt that the budget is "always" on time and "never" has caused a single problem.

Consider This: Find a New Angle

After the much-anticipated opening of a widened highway intended to ease massive traffic backups, the requisite press conference was scheduled. The conference was held on the side of the road, in front of a podium, and all the many officials who contributed to the construction of the new roadway gave each other verbal pats on the back. Yawn.

Each elected official was called up to speak, and in turn they thanked each other. Another podium, another boring press conference. But one official keyed in on a new angle: the weather.

The project had, in fact, been completed early due to a stretch of mild weather. Instead of thanking all the other politicians, as everyone else had, he offered his gratitude elsewhere.

"Thank you to Mother Nature," he said.

His comments were prominently featured in the article.

Brevity is key in all media outlets. You might have heard the term "sound bites." They are short quotes used in television news or highlighted in the copy of a newspaper or web article. They capture attention. Ronald Reagan was a master at such colorful comments.

If you want a better chance at having your quote used, make sure you throw in a few short, declarative comments with action and color. Or ask a short, colorful question that stirs some thoughtful responses from the news audience.

Attacking your competitor can almost guarantee you a prominent quote. But this is always risky business. When attacks are reported, they almost always reflect equally on both parties. Before spouting some clever verbal attack on your adversary, consider how it will reflect on you. Discuss these types of comments with colleagues, staff, and advisors and get their reaction before you use them. Look at every angle from which it will be interpreted. You never want to have to apologize for a comment that was out of line.

> ***Tips for Good Soundbites/Quotes:***
>
> *Keep them brief.*
>
> *Short, declarative sentences.*
>
> *Stay on point.*
>
> *Include action verbs or colorful adjectives.*
>
> *Say something slightly different from everyone else's comments.*

Anecdotes

Whenever you have the opportunity, throw in a brief anecdote. Such stories add a refreshing angle to any news piece. Colorful anecdotes could get you better press coverage and are often used as the opening of an article or news segment to grab an audience's attention. Reporters are always looking for anecdotes to liven up their stories.

But the basic rules apply, even with anecdotes—make sure the story is one that you don't mind sharing with the public. And don't use an anecdote that embarrasses or trashes a rival. That tactic only makes *you* look bad.

Remember, though, that this remains an interview. It's not cocktail party chatter. Keep your anecdotal material relative to the topic. Don't allow the conversation to drift into an area where you are encouraged to let your guard down.

Location, Location, Location

Where you schedule an interview is nearly as important as what you have to say. Before setting up an appointment for an interview, consider the setting.

If you have an on-camera interview scheduled, you need a setting that will reflect well on your image and your position. Sitting at a desk in an office is fine for some interviews but pretty boring generally. Consider the specifics of the story, your position within it, and find a suitable setting.

- Promoting your business? Set up near your business sign or banner. Stand in front of it for the photo or for the TV camera, and you instantly have free advertising.

- On the campaign trail? Sounds clichéd, but standing in front of a flag for the photo or camera has a subtle influence. If you are in a small town, stand near the local flag or banner. (The American flag typically works well too.) If there is a specific issue on which you are campaigning—assistance for seniors or environmental concerns—consider an appropriate setting to set the tone for your message.

- On the hot seat? Make sure the interview is in your arena— your home, your office. You'll be more comfortable on your own turf.

- Are you a non-profit administrator or community activist looking for some media promotion? If you have a very busy office, filled with volunteers and ringing phones, hold the interview there. If not, find a setting that illustrates the people or cause you are helping.

Sometimes, your office is indeed the best setting for on-camera interviews or discussions with the print media. Whenever you invite reporters to your office, check your desk before inviting them in. (Reporters tend to learn the tricky craft of reading upside down.) Then, close the door and don't take any calls. Noise and interruptions can disrupt the flow of the interview and lead to errors and miscommunication.

How to Handle the Ambush Interview

Unless you face a question on a topic that you are very familiar with, don't answer a question from a reporter who waits in the hall for you to leave your office—or, worse, hangs out in the parking lot near your car.

If a television camera catches you off guard, never put your hand up to block the lens. We have all witnessed that scene from the viewpoint of the audience, and it is, you must agree, not a pretty sight.

If you are surprised by an "ambush" interview:

Politely ask what the story is about. Ask the reporter how much time he would need to speak with you and when the deadline is.

Then agree to answer questions at an established time and place. Even if you allow yourself just ten minutes to prepare, you have given yourself time to collect your thoughts or consult a colleague or expert for advice.

If they insist, especially if they have a television camera rolling, just say you would be happy to accommodate their interview at another time. Often, a television reporter under tight deadline is just looking for a quick sound bite to accompany the story. Resist the temptation to toss out some unprepared or unflattering quote just to get rid of them.

Now, an ambush can be far more subtle than jumping out of the bushes near your car. A reporter sitting in the lobby of your building casually strikes up a conversation about a timely topic. Be careful what you say. A simple, casual discussion waiting for the elevator or in line for a cup of coffee can indeed be an interview—and you can, indeed, be quoted.

The matter of being "on the record" vs. being "off the record" is discussed at length further along in this book. I suggest that anyone who deals with the media read that section very carefully. Then, read it again. Most experienced news sources and even editors and reporters agree that this gray area between "on" and "off" the record can be problematic for both the source and the reporter.

Support Staff and Visuals

Always bring support staff and visuals along if they can help you convey your message. Visuals are a big deal for news outlets—print media need visuals to break up pages of copy. Television and Internet sites also need visuals to attract the audience's interest.

Before the interview, call in support staff or colleagues who may be able to augment the discussion. Have a briefing beforehand so all the parties get a handle on your main message points. Charts, graphs, photos, videos, or any other visual image can help get your story placed more prominently within the news item.

A good visual can make the difference in an editor choosing one story over the next. Remember, they need to sell papers, and they need to grab an audience to do it. Help them along by making your story more interesting with a visual.

Charts and graphs, particularly with regard to financial news and stories with loads of data, are essential. Long descriptions of a budget or financial outlook can be boring. A simple chart or pie graph can convey the financial picture in an eye-catching way that is simpler for the news audience to understand than lengthy explanations.

Support staff can help the reporter better understand the intricacies of any topic—just remind them all to ditch the technical jargon.

If some, or all, of the questions posed are outside your area of expertise, always have an expert with you for the interview, or refer the reporter to someone who can fill in the blanks following the interview. Trying to guess, or answer questions in a general way when you are not well informed, can be a big mistake.

Panel Interviews

Sometimes, several news sources representing different components of the companies or agencies involved in the news item will hold panel interviews. This can be effective. However, be very wary of the pronoun "we" in this situation. Speak very clearly when making comments—clearly explain each time you speak that the comment you make applies to you or to your specific department, not necessarily to everyone.

You might feel as though you are being overly repetitive if you identify your business or cause each time you address a question, but you are, in fact, helping the reporters keep the panel straight and the responses accurate.

When invited to participate in a panel interview, be sure to obtain a list of all the attendees and familiarize yourself with their titles and positions on issues to be discussed.

Consider This: Panel Discussions

A panel of officials from several separate municipalities were addressing a group of reporters; one official, who had been previously identified as representing one specific agency, responded to a question on policy. "We do it this way ..." he replied, explaining in detail the policy of his department. That particular policy, as it turned out, was not supported by some of the other officials on the panel. The reporters interpreted "we" collectively. The news stories that followed quoted the source as saying the policy was approved by all the agencies represented on the panel, causing confusion and fallout for the source.

Always avoid general pronouns like "we." Be clear to whom you are referring or whose behalf you are commenting, even if it means repeating yourself several times.

When an Unexpected Story Catches You Off Guard

You are in the midst of an interview about a relatively benign topic—you have your written bullet points, the reporter is asking a few general questions, and you are in your comfort zone, well informed, providing comprehensive answers. No stress.

Then, *BAM!* The reporter throws in a curve, an unexpected question on an unwelcome topic. When you agreed to the interview, they gave you no indication this issue would come up. You're furious.

Try not to act overly surprised; don't blurt out *"How did you find that out!"* Keep your composure. Reporters who ambush you with a topic are intentionally trying to get a reactionary response to liven up a story or to get a reaction without providing you the opportunity to craft an orchestrated response.

But they are also just doing their jobs. If they heard something newsworthy, they will want to report it. And asking you about might be the first step.

Take a deep breath and tell them you did not expect to discuss that issue. Remind them that they did not offer that topic for discussion when the interview was arranged, and set up another interview—even if it is fifteen minutes later. It will give you the opportunity to collect your thoughts and prepare a response.

Tip: The minute you lose your temper, or respond with emotion, you lose control of your positioning within the story.

Humor and a positive, optimistic response can catch some journalist's off-guard and change the angle of a story and your image.

A great example of how to change your image in the news with a simple comment occurred in early 2008 when a minor league baseball pitcher named Joe Odom was traded to another team for a dozen maple bats valued at a few hundred dollars. The unusual trade made national news. Odom appeared headed for an image of a loser, earning sympathy from some and ridicule from others. But Odom turned his image around with a single comment to reporters who asked him how he felt about being traded for equipment. "It'll make a better story when I make it to the Big Leagues" he said.

Odom won over the public. He didn't criticize the powers-that-be for the trade; he didn't complain or threaten to quit; he didn't cement his pitiful image with a negative reply. Instead, as the story made the rounds on hundreds on television stations and in countless newspapers, Odom was portrayed as an optimistic loyalist, a lover of the game of baseball, a guy who rolled with the punches, and a good sport. Journalists everywhere angled the story toward his optimistic perspective rather than the actual trade.

> ### *Tips for Remaining Calm When Caught Off Guard with a Sensitive Issue:*
>
> *Take two slow, deep breaths. Do not spit out an immediate response.*
>
> *Clarify the question or comment to make sure you understand what is being asked or implied.*
>
> *Use humor to defuse any growing anger.*
>
> *Briefly change the subject until you can process the comment/question.*
>
> *When possible, take a break, then take a walk or vent to a trusted friend or colleague before engaging in the interview.*
>
> *Never reply in anger, especially in an e-mail or on a television camera.*
>
> *Educate yourself with all the facts, then call or respond to the reporter in a cool, collected way. Hold your ground, be honest and stay good-natured.*

Tactful Atonement: Mea Culpa Tips

There is nothing worse, as a news source, than reading a news article and having the little hairs on the back of your neck begin to stand up, because you realize you may have provided the wrong information or given the wrong impression.

There are more examples of sources trying to find imprudent ways to cover their mistakes than I could ever fit in this book. But the bottom line is, when you make a mistake or provide bad info, just 'fess up.

Immediately obtain the right information, contact the reporter, apologize and provide the accurate details. If warranted, write a letter to the editor for publication or offer a comment on the news website, explaining your error and clarifying the information.

If the information impacts the public, write letters, make phone calls, and send e-mails to anyone whom you suspect might be affected by the misinformation. For example, if you have provided an incorrect date for a fund-raiser, and it was published or aired, ask for a guest list and personally contact everyone listed to correct the date. The news outlet also will likely provide the accurate details for its audience. But this should not stop you from making your own effort to get the correct details out there.

If you unintentionally reveal confidential information, call the reporter and ask if they can keep it under wraps. Journalists generally will work with you to some extent on such a problem.

For instance, I recall an official who inadvertently revealed the price of land being negotiated for preservation by the town. Developers were foaming at the mouth for the environmentally sensitive property. News of the negotiations leaked to the press. While confirming the preservation efforts to a reporter, a distracted official revealed the price offered by the municipality to the owner.

Negotiations on land purchases by municipalities can be kept confidential until a sales agreement is tendered, because once a proposed transaction price is published, developers have a jumping-off point to offer more money and possibly steal the land away from preservationists. We quickly called the editor and the reporter, explained the dilemma, and they agreed to cut the precise figure out of the story.

Sources make mistakes, and reporters are generally not unreasonable. Don't be afraid to admit an error and work out a solution.

There is a lot of value in a genuine apology, and a sincere *mea culpa* can work in your favor. Ignoring the error hurts your credibility as a news source and damages the news outlet's reputation. Foremost, journalists want accurate information, so if you provided incorrect material, correct it immediately.

Provided inaccurate information to a reporter?

1) Contact the reporter and editor immediately, briefly apologize, then provide the correct information.

2) Write a letter to the editor, e-mail a comment for the news website, or offer to prepare an oral statement for the radio or television news explaining your error and offering the accurate details.

3) Write letters, make phone calls, or send e-mails to anyone and everyone who may react to the misinformation.

Interviews on Complicated Issues

If you are facing a lengthy interview on a complicated issue, arrange to meet with the reporter and the editors too. In the industry, this setting is referred to as an *editorial board meeting*. At small papers, publishers might also participate. Sitting down with the entire editorial board will help flesh out the topic along with all its history and the ancillary details. With more than one set of ears listening to your responses and explanations, the story likely will be more accurate and complete.

You may have to do several interviews; it is unlikely that reporters and editors from competing news outlets will all agree to meet you together. So schedule the interviews at the news outlets' offices, all on the same day if possible, so the facts are clear in your mind.

Meeting with the editors as well as the reporters is a good option when the story is complicated, you have a long history to explain, or when you can't possible narrow down your responses to a few basic message points.

If necessary, bring along support staff and any type of visual images, charts or reports that may help the journalists to better understand the issue. Keep your support team to two or three people.

When the interview concludes, be sure to provide contact information so the journalists can reach you to clarify any misunderstandings or if they have any follow-up questions.

Whenever dealing with reporters on complicated matters, provide as much written material as possible. Provide them with charts, list of names, and a timeline of events. Try to pare down the issue, to quantify and explain through graphics. Make sure you, or your spokesperson, are available for follow up interviews.

Wrap-Up: Ten Questions To Ask Yourself When a Reporter Calls for an Interview:

1. What is my role within this story?

2. How can I position myself within the context?

3. Do I have a grasp of the exact topic and angle?

4. What are my three main message points?

5. What do I anticipate them asking me? Who, what, where, when and why?

6. Do I have all the facts I need to answer fully?

7. Could there be any tricky questions—areas of discussion outside my comfort zone?

8. Where should I hold the interview? Will there be a television camera or photographer?

9. What is their deadline?

10. Do I need support staff? Visuals? Charts and graphs?

Step Two:
Where Are the Land Mines?

There are plenty of landmines when dealing with the media. Understanding where they are and how you might unintentionally trigger them is the key to getting solid and accurate press coverage.

By understanding the boundaries and by staying focused, you can avoid most of the potential difficulties that come along with interacting with the media.

What "Off the Record" Really Means

If you gather ten reporters and ask them to write down their interpretation of "off the record," you are likely to get several different responses—perhaps ten. Each reporter might handle OTR information in his or her own way.

Some reporters and editors define "off the record" in its strictest terms: anything you say to a reporter in that context will not be used or repeated in any way. It goes entirely into the vault—it is strictly confidential.

But in my 12 years' combined experience on both sides of the media desk, I rarely encountered "off the record" to be quite so stringent. In fact, typically there is a lot more gray area and different interpretations depending on a number of factors. Some interpret it as meaning they can report the information, as long as they don't reveal you as its source. Others will repeat the information to others, protecting your identity, in an effort to confirm it for publication.

Tip: If you go off the record, discuss with the reporter how they interpret OTR and what they will specifically do to protect your identity.

I have found that if reporters have some pertinent piece of information related to their beats, at some point they will want to use it. Journalists never want to be accused of covering anything up. Hoarding information just isn't in their nature. Besides, their job description is reporting, not simply knowing.

For most news sources in most situations, I suggest a cautionary stance when considering off-the-record discussions. Never assume that your identity will be protected entirely or that the information you provide is classified. "Off the record" is not the same as confidential discussions you may have with your colleagues or your attorney. (Having said that, I know a reporter who protected her source all the way to the Pennsylvania Supreme Court. She won the case and the source was never revealed. As I said, OTR is different with every reporter.)

But let me repeat: You are speaking to the press. Their professional obligation is to get information to the public. OTR information provides reporters with a blueprint for the story. It can serve as a catalyst for obtaining additional information from another source, or for getting another source to confirm *on* the record the information you provided *off* the record.

OTR can get you into trouble, legally and otherwise. A good reporter likely will honor his or her end of the bargain, and your name won't be linked with the information. Still, do not be lured into a sense of security that the information will not be reported at all; do not think that your name as the source will not be provided to an editor or publisher, or even to the others in the newsroom.

To be on the safe side, just don't go there. If a reporter asks to go off the record, consider the topic being discussed and your position. Unless it is an extreme situation, just stay on the record. If you represent an organization, municipality or company where confidentiality rules have been clearly established, clam up immediately.

Consider the following before going off the record with the press: Will your job or reputation be at risk if you are revealed as the source? Will someone else's job or reputation be at risk if the information is published? Will a project or program be jeopardized if this information is revealed prematurely? Why do you want to provide the information at all?

Best bet? Stay on the record during interviews.

Anonymity and the Newsroom

If you find yourself frequently serving as an anonymous source for a reporter, take into consideration the likelihood that 1) others in the newsroom know you're the source, or 2) your name will be inadvertently revealed. Then consider how that revelation will impact your position, your reputation, someone else's position, a project, and so on.

Reporters within the newsroom meet regularly to catch up on the pending stories. These meetings are considered confidential within most newsrooms. But even if the reporter you deal with hasn't revealed your name within that confidential setting, his or her colleagues might have guessed who you are, based on that reporter's beat and known contacts. You might feel secure that the actual reporter you deal with will keep your identity a secret—but how sure are you about the others in the newsroom? Do you even know them?

Also, bear in mind the massive amounts of information reporters and editors deal with each day. I have been shown articles that I had written while a reporter, and I have no recollection of the article, the source, the story. Some reporters write dozens of articles a week, interview hundreds of sources in a year. Their investment in the facts of a particular story can be fleeting—and certainly they are never as invested as you are.

Are you prepared to handle any fallout should you be ousted as the anonymous source a week from now? A month from now? A year?

Reporters are generally as careful as they can be to protect sources, but in my experience, especially in magnified beats—small towns, political arenas, etc.—the names of anonymous sources tend to get out. And, again, it's often inadvertent.

When I took over a stormy political beat from a reporter who moved on to another publication, she left some of her notes for me. Inside were lists of very controversial "anonymous" quotes she had used in past articles. Beside the quotes were initials—unusual initials.

I instantly knew who the source was, and over the next few weeks I intentionally sought out that official, developed a casual, professional relationship, gained that official's trust, and within months I had my own leak.

Reporters need sources; they work hard to develop solid relationships and to honor all confidences. But information sometimes gets out, especially within the newsroom.

When Are You *On* the Record? Always

If you bump into a reporter at happy hour, or at the gas station; if you are in line behind him at the supermarket; if you are just chatting with her in any casual situation—consider yourself on the record. They are reporters. They report. And they are always looking for a story.

Tip: You can find yourself quoted in the newspaper after a simple remark made when you assumed the reporter was "off duty." Good reporters are never off duty.

Unless you have an established relationship with a specific reporter and you are clear that the discussion is not for publication, be wary of what you say. Talk about the weather, the Mets, anything but your newsworthy job or position.

When I was reporting on local government for a weekly newspaper, I would head over to the Town Hall on quiet days at the newsroom and just sit on a bench in a busy upstairs hallway. I would bring my notes to write the first draft of a story, or some books for research. Staff there knew me and would regularly stop by, sit down and chitchat. They got a brief respite from their busy workdays, and I got plenty of tips for stories. Reporters can't cover a beat by sitting at their desks waiting for the phone to ring. They must get out into the community and talk to people, to sources. So when you bump into them somewhere, always consider yourself to be on the record.

While on the topic of "off" and "on" the record, let me address an issue I encountered several times in both of my capacities, as reporter and as spokesperson. Never invite a reporter to sit in on a private meeting or brainstorming session and then try to direct what is "on" and "off" the record. A source cannot expect a reporter to sit in on a meeting and only report the parts that the source wants published. If you ask the press to participate in private meetings, you take your chances that any or all of it will be reported. If a participant misspeaks or reveals information you had hoped to keep quiet, that is just too bad if you invited the press to sit in.

I would advise against inviting reporters to brainstorming sessions. Too often, speculation, opinion, or a preliminary suggestion will land in a headline, only to be interpreted by the readers or audience as a "done deal."

Consider This: On The Record?

During a break at a municipal public meeting, a reporter who was visiting the ladies room overheard two elected officials harshly criticizing a colleague. To the surprise and dismay of these two officials, their unkind and inflammatory comments appeared in the next edition of the local weekly newspaper.

Any journalist will tell you that the reporter had every right to report the newsworthy comments she overheard.

The reporter was covering her beat—the municipal meeting. The provocative conversation played out between two elected officials in a public building, albeit in a restroom. It was perfectly acceptable for the reporter to tell the public what she overheard.

The point is, once again, that reporters are always on duty, and their job is to fill in the public about what is going on in their community. And even in the restroom.

Unnamed Sources and Attribution

Another pesky three-word phrase—"not for attribution"—can likewise be problematic.

If a reporter suggests that you speak "not for attribution," this means that he or she will include the information that the source tells them but will not assign the source's name to it in the article.

There are a few things to consider if you are presented with this situation. How many people know this information? Will you be pegged as the source? Examine your motives under this scenario: Why put it out there at all if you are hesitant to have your name attached?

If a reporter wants to use you as an "unnamed source," ask *specifically* how he or she will identify you. To establish credibility, he or she might attribute the quote or information to "a person associated with the matter," or "an elected official," or "a high-ranking staff member."

Giving information on "background" is similar: a reporter can use the general information in explanatory paragraphs to educate the reader/audience but will not attribute it to you as the news source. But be cautious providing sensitive material under "not for attribution" or "background" agreements—it isn't worth it if it comes back to haunt you or hurt your company or office.

Once again, ask yourself the question: If you unwilling to attach your name to it, then why provide the information? In some cases, if you believe a reporter should have the background information, but you don't want to be the one to reveal it, then direct him or her to a more appropriate source who might be willing to provide the details.

Avoid the Dual Named *and* Unnamed Source Trick

If you turn down a request from a reporter to be used as an unnamed source, beware a follow-up tactic he or she might suggest.

In some cases, reporters will quote a source in a story with a benign comment, then use that same person as an unnamed source later in the story. A reporter might sell this tactic as a means of protecting your identity: If a source is openly quoted in one part of a story, it is less likely that person would be suspected as the confidential source cited in the same story.

It's an effective tactic to some degree, but be cautious for all the same reasons outlined in the sections above related to *off the record* and *unnamed sources.*

Under this scenario, you will come across as sneaky if you are revealed as the confidential source.

Remain Silent During Those Awkward Pauses

Answering more than the question requires is the most frequent error made by inexperienced interviewees.

Delving into topics outside the parameters of a question opens the door for confusion. Listen carefully and answer only what is asked; don't volunteer information unless it enhances your position.

Be concise and respond in one or two sentences. Then wait for the follow-up question.

Anyone who has ever testified in court has been briefed by an attorney on how to answer *just* the question asked. Think about the question and the response. If you don't understand it, ask the reporter to repeat or rephrase the question.

Reporters looking for an angle or secondary story will sometimes intentionally wait a few seconds after you respond. Silence is awkward in any professional situation. Interviewees will have a natural tendency to mitigate the tension by elaborating on their previous comment. The awkward pause is a tried-and-true journalistic tactic and can be an effective way to obtain additional information. Wait out the silence, and the reporter will move on to the next question.

Just answer the question asked. Brief, concise, straightforward.

Fishing Expeditions: Baited into Giving the Story

This is the most common "oops" I have heard from inexperienced officials who have found that they inadvertently gave a reporter a story: If a reporter contacts you about a topic that is completely off-limits, don't say anything at all. Even a seemingly benign comment can give the reporter a jumping-off point to do a story.

Here's the hypothetical scenario: An employee of an organization or municipality is suspected of accepting bribes. This information is strictly confidential until the investigation is completed. A reporter has inkling that something is going on but has no starting point for any type of story.

The reporter calls Source #1 and tosses out some vague bait: *"I heard what is going on with Joe Smith."*

Knowing this is a sensitive matter, Source #1 replies, "*I can't comment until we get more information.*"

HOOKED! Source #1 just gave the reporter a story by confirming that there is indeed a problem and then stating that information is forthcoming, suggesting some type of investigation is underway.

Then the reporter calls Source #2 and asks for confirmation of Source #1's comment that additional information about Mr. Smith is forthcoming. Source #2 says, "*No comment until the investigation is complete*"—verifying there is an ongoing investigation.

Both sources have given the reporter a jumping-off point, and a pretty juicy headline to boot: "Investigation Underway on Joe Smith; Officials Nervously Await Outcome."

When confronted with a vague comment or question on a sensitive matter, always ask the reporter what they are referring to and specifically what they have heard. If you can't avoid the conversation completely, simply answer questions with your own questions.

For example, Source #1 should have responded to the initial bait with, "*What do you mean?*"

The reporter may have kept pressing on: "*I mean, what is going on with Joe Smith? Doesn't sound too good.*"

"*What specifically are you referring to? What doesn't sound good?*" would be your next response.

Now, the persistent reporter may take a leap and throw out a guess. They have nothing to lose. "*I mean, that he is in the trouble he's in. Come on, you can talk to me. We'll go off the record.*"

"*Let's stay on the record. What trouble are you talking about?*" Continue until the reporter gives in. Without a jumping-off point, the reporter can't produce a story.

When Sarcasm Bites Back

Sarcasm is a great tool in some types of discussions. It can be used to deflect, offset tension, define your personality, make people laugh.

But if it's your natural tendency to be sarcastic or cheeky, quell that impulse when dealing with the media, especially with print reporters.

Tongue-in-cheek statements never read well. In fact, the fallout from facetious remarks can be disastrous. Keep your answers straight and serious. If the situation itself is humorous, a light joke can sometimes work. Sarcasm rarely does.

This is particularly important to remember if responding in writing in an e-mail or a letter to the editor. I recall damage control for days over a message written with a facetious slant. The official writing the piece considered it amusing and assumed the readers would get the irony and, subsequently, his point. Instead, people were offended, and his adversaries used the message as ammo.

Self-deprecation can create a similar problem. Comments can easily be twisted when they are truncated for the news. Avoid self-deprecatory remarks, or you may end up with a quote that ends with "he admitted." Whenever a reporter uses "admitted" or "maintained" near your comments, it has an inherently negative connotation. Always speak of yourself and your company or cause in positive terms.

Consider This: One Sarcastic Remark

A personable elected official was haunted for years by a quote in the local newspaper that he maintained was simple sarcasm.

In the midst of a public fervor over land preservation issues, an elected official told a local reporter that there was plenty of land left just waiting to be developed. The firestorm of criticism over that comment lasted throughout the remainder of his term of office. He was strongly criticized by a community very protective of its remaining natural resources.

He couldn't deny that he said it; indeed, he did say it. But he maintained that it was intended facetiously. The problem was that the comment didn't come across that way in the context of a serious article.

There is a difference between humor and sarcasm. The former can work for news sources in some circumstances; the latter never works in print and only sometimes on camera.

"What If" and "Rumors Are Swirling" Questions

Never respond to a "What if ..." question. Never answer if asked to speculate on an outcome or comment on rumors.

There can be fallout from answering a hypothetical question. If you are wrong, you can be accused of being misleading. If it turns out you are correct, someone might suspect you had inside information that nobody else had.

I regularly fielded "What do you think will happen if ..." questions. I always answered with the same response: "Not sure. What do *you* think will happen?"

Or just say, "I guess we will all see what happens when it happens, and we'll talk about the next step then."

If the reporter persists, simply say you do not care to speculate.

The "What Happens Next" Question

To fully answer the 5 W's (who, what, where, when and why?) reporters will often want to know the next step—a timeline or the follow-up plan of action. If you have a solid set of sequential events in mind, it may be your natural inclination to respond. Seems harmless.... and often it is, but not always.

Think carefully before providing too many specifics here. I recently watched a law enforcement union representative being interviewed on camera following the announcement of a forced retirement plan implemented by municipal officials. The union rep was outraged at the unexpected forced retirement and while speaking at length to a television reporter he offered every detail of the union's legal plans to reverse the policy. And as he spoke I could envision the municipal attorneys taking notes on his comments, then jumping into a pre-emptive legal strategy of their own. Be careful not to give your adversaries and competitors your game plan. Remember, when you speak a reporter, you speak to everyone.

Timelines can be tricky too. Avoid providing an absolute with regard to the deadline for a project or investigation. Reporters like time frames but providing specific dates is not always in the source's best interest. "The project will be finished in July" is a dangerous response. That may be the outcome you expect at the time of the interview but if there are unforeseen delays, the project is considered overdue on August 1 because of your statement. "We hope to see the end result sometime this summer" is a better response.

The Unwelcome or Unexpected Story

Sometimes you eat the bear, and sometimes the bear eats you. Sometimes you are looking for a news story, and sometimes a news story is looking for you.

In the latter case, if a story you had hoped wouldn't get out is about to be leaked, get out ahead of it. Every time. Preemptive strike.

If there is something in your background, or some negative issue related to the news story, present it on your own terms right away. And present it completely—don't leave out some details and cross your fingers, hoping they won't be uncovered later.

It's tempting, when faced with an issue we'd rather not see on the front page, to hide and hope it blows over. But this only accomplishes two things: you appear to be hiding, which you are; and your adversaries benefit by having their quotes in the story while you have none.

When you suspect that someone is poised to reveal some bit of news that you'd hoped would be hidden away forever, beat them to the punch. Call a meeting with the press; bring along support troops if possible. If you need to offer a mea culpa, offer it fast.

If you are beaten to the punch, and the media finds out first, you will instantly find yourself on the defensive. Keep your composure and your responses honest but brief, especially if you have not had time to carefully prepare your reply. Consider the seriousness of the issue and the impact on your colleagues, family or business.

If the issue is a public matter, you must provide every detail and be as accommodating as possible in providing follow-up information.

If it is a personal matter, you have far more leverage, and you can be selective about what your reveal.

When George W. Bush was caught off guard during his first campaign for president by a question about his drug use as a young man, his response was a clever one in terms of a news source trying to deflect and control a story. "When I was young and irresponsible, I was young and irresponsible," he said.

His comment did not confirm anything specific, but it hinted that he made mistakes. He followed up with a series of comments urging Baby Boomers who made mistakes in their teens and 20s to make an effort to steer their children away from making the same mistakes.

The quote didn't make the story go away, but he managed to diffuse what could have blown up into a story that might have ruined his campaign.

Information coming directly from you is always the best scenario in a bad situation.

If asked to respond to a negative story, consider who or what the news is specifically about, and whether what you are saying is true beyond any doubt, before replying.

For example, if reporters indeed appear to have accurate facts for a negative story—let's say, a business is financially strapped for many reasons other than the declining economy, and a group of people are about to be let go from prominent positions/jobs—and you are asked to respond. Consider the following:

The bad news is about you: Be honest, concise and direct. Don't ignore the issue, but don't harp on it either. *"Thank you for your concern. I will miss the position and the people, but I am looking forward to the next chapter in my life."* 'Nuff said. Don't blame, criticize or come across as bitter.

The bad news is about others in your company or department: Be very careful. Get advice from your boss or an attorney if you are required to address the issue. Discern what is public information and what is private information before responding. Never speculate about why this occurred or what will happen next. If you are not the appropriate spokesperson, don't comment at all: *"You should speak to them about this matter—I am not the appropriate person to speak with."*

The news is about a family member: When dealing with personal issues, you have much more leverage to avoid commenting at all. Simply say that you have no public comment; maybe add that you will support your spouse/parent/child/sibling in whatever he or she decides to do next. There are very few situations when you are obligated to reply to the media with regard to a matter related to family members. Don't feel pressured to respond. This is a rare situation when you can get away with "no comment" without coming off in a bad light.

The news is about an opponent or competitor: Never gloat. Offer very little. Your own image will depend on your response. *"I wish them well in their future endeavors."* If asked to speculate about whether their misfortune will benefit you ... never say yes. Switch the topic over to your own accomplishments and try to gain some positive coverage for yourself without ever criticizing your ill-fated opponent.

No Comment

A lawyer colleague of mine encouraged the liberal use of this response. *"No comment"* is a full sentence, she would advise her clients who had been approached by the media. Lawyers will do that. And that is why, sometimes, they are considered poor news sources.

But other than lawyers, few would agree that this is a beneficial response under most circumstances. Indeed, there are some instances where you should not be quoted: litigation, personnel/staff issues, contract or other negotiations, and personal matters outside the scope of your professional position. Under these scenarios, indicate that you cannot comment because of pending litigation or because you don't want to jeopardize a negotiation by revealing too much in the media. Then promise to comment at a later date when the issue resolves or concludes.

Tip: If you stick with the two-word reply "no comment," you will just end up sounding uncooperative and as if you are hiding something.

There are plenty of ways to say "no comment" without uttering those two inflammatory words. Simply explain why you cannot, at this time, offer background or quotes.

Phrases to use instead of "*no comment*":

"I must learn more about this myself, and I will comment when I have the entire picture."

"I can't comment because this is a confidential (litigation matter, personnel issue, contract negotiation), but once it is resolved I will be happy to speak to you."

"I am taking this very seriously and I will comment when I am able to do so—please check back with me later/tomorrow/next week."

Little White Lies

Your credibility is your number-one asset as a news source. Honesty should be your number-one priority.

Don't lie—a simple tenet of life that we learn in nursery school. Yet we all do it from time to time. It is human nature.

But when dealing with the media, never try to pull one over on them. This tactic is always a mistake. If a reporter discovers that you have been less than truthful with him or her, you will be labeled as a liar and your credibility will be permanently shot. You will likely not be used as a news source again, and even if you are, everything you say will be verified and double-checked.

Always keep two things in mind: a reporter might already know the answer to the question he or she asking; and the reporter likely will interview other sources and pose the same questions. Conflicting responses will provide motivation for further digging, and your lie could be exposed. (This includes hyperbole, too. Remember that exaggeration is, in fact, a lie.)

Finally, remember that reporters may not reveal that you are giving them info they already have—they want to hear your take on a situation they are familiar with or they could simply be protecting other source. Acting surprised over info they already have is a common journalistic practice.

Phrases To Avoid: These phrases can affect your credibility, even if it is on a subliminal level.

"*To be honest ...*" or "*To tell you the truth ...*" It sounds as though you haven't previously been straight with a reporter.

"*On the QT ...*" or "*Between you and me ...*" Nothing is on the QT with the press. You should be comfortable with whatever you say appearing in the news story.

Unsure About the Angle? You Are on a Slippery Slope

You are on a slippery slope if you don't have a firm grasp of what the story is about. You leave yourself wide open to being baited into saying something that later might appear to you to be out of context, because you were out of sync with the reporter.

If the topic is a broad one, be sure to ask *before* the interview begins about the angle of the story. If the interview begins and you are still unsure, start asking questions of your own—get a handle on the scope of the story. Once you have a firm grasp of the angle, you can prepare your message points and find an advantageous starting point for the discussion.

Consider This: When the Angle Changes

A reporter told an official he was writing a story on land preservation—a good topic, and the local municipality had been successfully preserving farms and parks for years. The official agreed to an interview and commented at length, anticipating a positive story on preservation efforts.

The next issue of the paper featured an article about developers building before the municipality had the chance to preserve the land, a sort of "the officials are dragging their heels with preservation" angle. The official's name was all over the article. In fact, since he was the only source quoted, he fielded all the fallout.

Friendships with Reporters…Another Slippery Slope

Reporters covering a regular beat will try to make connections and develop relationships with regular sources. They may call every few days, meet you for lunch or drinks, spend an hour discussing the Yankees.

Remember, they have many sources like you, and the parameters in their world are usually pretty clear. But from the perspective of the source, the lines can become blurred. Always keep the relationship professional. They will.

Once you begin viewing a reporter as a friend, confidante or public relations outlet, you are setting yourself up for mistakes, disappointment and poor coverage.

Media is a game of mutual support. Reporters need sources. They have to be personable, charming, and hang around you and other sources to cover a regular beat. The bottom line is that they are watchdogs, and if they do their job right, when the news about you is unflattering they will print it.

So, don't develop a false sense of security. Some sources are genuinely shocked when a member of the media they had grown fond of did his or her job by reporting something negative. Keep the boundaries clear and remember that a journalist's professional obligation is to report all newsworthy events.

Establish a friendly rapport with reporters, a casual, professional relationship similar to that you have with your boss or clients. A good relationship with journalists can provide you with productive feedback and perhaps even tips on developing stories. You may get advance notice of pending attacks from your competitors and a better understanding of the media's perspective on your projects. But always remember the distinction between your goals and that of the reporters.

To explain this through one of my own experiences: A source in a social setting, angry with her boss for personal reasons, mentioned in passing something he had done in his professional capacity that was less than ethical. As a reporter, it put me in a terrible position. Her boss was an official whose office I covered on my beat, but the information was not easily verified. She told me in a fit of anger, then she and the boss made their personal amends and it was never mentioned again. I poked around a bit, but without information only she could provide, there was no way to verify it. I'm sure she never realized it, but if could have verified that information, I would have reported the ethical breach.

Damage Control: Bouncing Back

You have made a big blunder, a messy newsworthy one, and now you are waiting for a reporter to call. This isn't just a little goof. You have compromised your credibility or the reputation of your cause or company and you have no choice but to address it publicly. How do you handle it?

If you can, get out there with your admission and apology right away. *Act* on presenting a major mea culpa before you are forced to *react* to an accusation from an opponent or a reporter.

The first thing to remember is not to make excuses. If you dance around the issue and offer excuses instead of an apology, the damage to your reputation can be compounded. Own up to the error with mild humility and a sincere apology but without justifications and rationalizations. Apologize, explain, and then move on. Do it quickly and keep it brief. Don't kick yourself too much; just prepare yourself with the facts and apologize.

Don't try and cover it up, don't avoid the media hoping it will go away and don't blame someone else if it really is your fault. Never trash the person who revealed the error.

For instance, if you erred in a budget and there is a big deficit, you should apologize and explain plans to correct the matter. Keep the reporter apprised of all the follow-up strategies to get the budget back in the black.

How you handle yourself with the media following a big goof-up guides the subsequent coverage and can permanently shape your image. If the news is so big, so bad, that it could have a dramatic negative impact in your job, your campaign, or your business, assemble a few trusted advisors and set a crisis management plan into action. (See detailed section on crisis management in the last chapter.)

Consider This: Failure To Make Proper Amends

An amiable lawyer was running for local political office. Just weeks before the election, he was spotted by a homeowner defacing a political lawn sign—a sign promoting his opponent. The homeowner contacted the police, and, later, reporters.

All in all, a messy and embarrassing situation for the candidate, a lawyer who was campaigning on his reputation and business savvy. News reports abounded, he was widely criticized for his shenanigans.

When reporters called for his reaction, he admitted the offense and offered a lukewarm apology. He then inexplicably criticized the homeowner for her reaction. This was an extremely poor reaction, one that did not help him to repair his tattered reputation, and, in fact, hurt him further.

From a PR standpoint, there are five steps the candidate might have taken to help mend his image and prove that he truly regretted the prank.

1. Before calling back the reporter, call the homeowner, and his opponent, offering a sincere apology.

2. Offer to pay for a replacement sign.

3. Offer to make a generous donation to the local charity of the homeowner's choice—from his own account, not from his political contributions account.

4. Call the reporter and recount all of the above, adding a further apology to the community for his behavior.

5. Write a letter to the editor for publication recounting the apology and include mention of the donation to the homeowner's charity of choice.

These five actions would not have erased the mistake, but they would be interpreted as a major mea culpa and a step toward making up for a big goof.

Don't Be Drawn into Back-and-Forth Quote Wars

No matter what your position, or who your adversaries are, try not to let a reporter draw you into a back-and-forth quote war. Stating a contrary position is fine, but focus on your own stance and your own goals.

A good quote war in the paper can liven up a story. Some reporters love them and intentionally bait their sources into this type of discussion. But it rarely sheds positive light on either of the sources.

There is always a lot of push and pull in the news. Businesses compete, political opponents toss out verbal salvos, police and judges field unkind comments from those who feel aggrieved. But remember you can disagree yet remain courteous.

When I served as the spokesperson for a high-profile elected official, one particular reporter seemed to enjoy pulling my boss into quote wars with another elected official. The two officials had a history of taking contrary stances on issues but nonetheless had a cordial relationship—until they started reading each other's quotes.

Before long, they were firing off terse memos and intentionally undercutting one another in the political arena. The tension lasted for years and produced numerous colorful stories—none of which reflected well on either politician.

The entire ruckus began with a few quotes incited by an overzealous reporter who called one official and said, "He said this about you! Can you believe that! Do you have a response?" Then she called the other. "He said your comments were this, that and the other! What is your reaction?"

The real news got lost, became murky, was largely ignored. The news stories focused on the war of words instead.

When this happens—and it will if you allow yourself to be pulled into ongoing quote wars—it becomes a problem with a long shelf life. Real news is lost in a barrage of controversies and conflict. Misunderstandings brew, misinformation flies, and the actual news—what the public deserves to read or hear—becomes skewed.

Hints About Upcoming "Big" Stories

This may seem like a no-brainer, but I can't tell you how many times I have heard an official, law enforcement officer or politician tease a reporter with hints of a big story about to break. Comments like "*You have no idea what kind of big story you're going to have in a few days,*" or "*Just wait—something big is about to blow*" won't just pique reporters' curiosity—it will motivate them to find out right away what they are missing.

I got one of my biggest stories this way. Within 24 hours of a source suggesting that in a "few weeks" I would have a big story to report, I had broken the news that a longstanding, respected official was being investigated on bribery charges. The story landed on the front page just days later, before the grand jury even handed down an indictment.

So, unless you are *intentionally* trying to get the reporter to poke around, lay off the hints and innuendos. Most reporters wont wait for the story to come to them—they will begin asking around immediately, hitting every one of their sources until they find out to what you were referring. Curiosity is a big part of most reporters' nature. They don't like unanswered questions. When there is big news floating around, many people are generally bursting at the seams to spill it—and reporters are well aware of this. It is actually not difficult to get confidential information. So, never tease a reporter about a story that is brewing but not yet ready to be made public.

Step Three:
The Proper Care and Feeding of Your Media Inquiries

How you manage your press inquiries is an important step toward gaining better press coverage. Set clear guidelines for assistants, family members or anyone else who takes messages from reporters. Do you want to be notified right away? Can it wait? Do you want it passed on to a spokesperson? If there are times when you don't want to speak to the reporter, tell your message-takers exactly what you want them to say. A simple "unavailable at the moment" is probably your best bet.

If you are the spokesperson for a company, non-profit, law enforcement agency, or elected official, you must always have a clear understanding of the preferred agenda and message. Schedule regular meetings with your boss or supervisor to make sure you are on the same page. As spokesperson, it is your responsibility to stay on top of the information. Don't wait for data to find their way to you. Be proactive.

Who is the Spokesperson in Your Absence?

Don't underestimate the importance of this decision. If you deal with the media on a regular basis, consider very carefully who will speak to the press in your absence.

Designate *one* person to speak for you. Hold regular briefings with your spokesperson to make sure he or she has a clear understanding of the facts and of your position—never assume that they have all the facts and grasp all the nuances. A good spokesperson must have the ability to articulate your position and stay on message. Choose someone who is personable and likeable. Your spokesperson should be well informed and charismatic.

Direct all staff to give media messages to your appointed spokesperson. Remind the others never to casually chat with reporters who call seeking interviews. It is imperative that everyone on your team who interacts with reporters understands the concepts detailed in this book. Many people who have never dealt with the media don't grasp the watchdog status and could inadvertently provide information that lands on the front page.

For instance, a receptionist for the CEO of a large company in financial trouble took a call from a reporter one morning. Her boss was not yet in the office and she quipped, "He's always late." The reporter keyed in, turned on the charm, and began commiserating in an attempt to draw out additional information on the whereabouts of her boss. Soon, he had two pages of notes about the official, who routinely showed up for work at lunchtime or skipped work entirely. The reporter had a front-page story, one that included quotes from the receptionist, who had no idea when she was chatting away that in fact she was acting as a news source and was on the record.

Tip: Make sure your staff is aware that any comment they make to a reporter could be included in the news story.

In my own experience, a receptionist in our office once casually offered her opinion on a hotly debated issue. Her opinion differed from our boss. Her comments didn't make it into the final cut of the story, but they undermined our boss's stance. Certainly, we all have the right our own opinions, but casually sharing them with the press was not in the administration's best interest.

If your spokesperson has a strong opinion or position that differs from yours, talk it over with him or her at length before any reporters call seeking comment on the matter. Don't let an opposing opinion seep in, sending mixed messages to the media. If your spokesperson can't clearly articulate your stance because of a personal opinion that conflicts with yours, you must do all the talking.

Even if you have a professional spokesperson, it is important to talk to the press yourself on a regular basis. Reporters develop a healthy skepticism about PR reps, and if the rep's is the only voice a reporter ever hears, the reporter may lose interest or become a bit cynical about you or your cause.

Handling Incoming Media Messages

Establish clear guidelines with your colleagues, assistants or family members about how you want to receive your media inquiries. Some sources collect them during the course of the day and return them all at a set time. Other sources prefer to handle them as they come in. Still others want to set up face-to-face interviews. And some direct support staff to return a call to provide the basic background, and then call in quotes when they get the chance.

Decide how you want to handle your incoming media messages and make sure your support staff understands how to provide you with the messages.

Also, make sure your staff or family members know exactly what should be included in the message—a detailed topic for discussion, the reporter's deadline and contact numbers, for example.

Some news sources use a daily log to record all incoming calls from reporters. Each day they set aside time to return press calls. These logs are filed so there is a record of every reporter the source has spoken to and every topic discussed.

Prepare a list of each reporter's name, beat, deadline, contact number and editor's name. (Update it every few months—staff turnover at newspapers can be rapid.) If a new reporter is assigned to regularly cover your department or business, schedule a "get-to-know-you" briefing over lunch or breakfast. During the briefing, go over your background and any basic details that the reporter will need to know. Provide lists with correct spellings, titles, departments and contact numbers to give the reporter a good base for coverage.

The News Hog

Don't be a news hog. You might want your name and company in the news as often as possible, but trying to handle media inquiries outside your area of expertise is a mistake.

If the media are looking for comment on an issue that falls within your comfort zone, then by all means do the interview. If not, either refer them to someone else or obtain the information and then call them back. By agreeing to an interview better suited to a colleague or even a competitor, you risk providing bad information, which will result in an inferior article. This will not go unnoticed by the reporter and the editors. You could be considered an unreliable source, and you won't be the one they call for future stories.

Multiple Requests for Interviews on the Same Topic

If you receive multiple requests for interviews on an identical topic and you are tight on time, by all means schedule collective interviews. It does not have to be a formal press conference; in fact, it is better if it is scheduled as a less formal discussion.

Invite the reporters in at the same time, set up in a comfortable conference room, and have all the backup reports, releases, photos and support staff available. If a reporter prefers a phone interview, you can conference them in. Preset a time limit for the collective interview, and then set aside two or three minutes for each individual reporter following the group discussion. (It's best not to reveal in advance that you will allow them each their own time slot at the end of the collective interview, or they will likely hold all their questions for the one-on-one time.)

Ask your spokesperson or an assistant to sit in, and if you are unavailable for follow-up calls, direct them to your assistant. Make sure your designated spokesperson participated in the collective interview and has access to all the relevant information.

If you regularly deal with the same group of reporters, scheduling weekly collective update interviews can be a big time-saver. I have had editors balk at this suggestion that all the reporters from competing news outlets meet and interview together, but that is simply their competitive nature—usually, it's the most productive news source that complains. I also found fewer reporting errors when we held casual interviews/discussions to update reporters on all the issues each week.

There will still be follow-up calls and new topics that come up after the meeting, but you won't have to repeat the basics and background six separate times in one day for six different reporters.

When and Where to Schedule Interviews

Face-to-face interviews: Schedule interviews in person on the more important topics. This is particularly important if you are actively promoting an issue or presenting information on a new idea or complicated issue.

Don't get caught in the routine of inviting a reporter to sit by your desk for every interview. Talk a walk, schedule the interview at the park or on the beach, meet for coffee. Change the location, especially when you frequently deal with the same reporter. Don't always be the "suit" behind the desk for every interview. (See "location" tips in Part One.)

Phone interviews: Interviews over the phone are fine for answering quick questions or providing background information. But any discussion with the media expected to last longer than ten minutes, or which requires visual aids, should be conducted in person. If you are unfamiliar with the reporter, ask if you are being taped. Recording interviews is a common practice with many reporters, but it is in the source's best interest to know when conversations are being taped.

At meals: Scheduling a lengthy interview—or a "get-to-know-you" interview—at breakfast or lunch is often a good arena. When I was reporting, I took my regular sources to lunch every month or so to catch up on the recent news or to cover several time-consuming topics at once.

But there are a few things to consider. First, look around to see who is seated near you. If you are providing sensitive information, don't let your guard down just because you and the reporter are chowing down on turkey sandwiches. Keep in mind, the reporter is still on duty, and your conversation is on the record. Also, set parameters in advance for who pays for the meal; splitting the check is your best option and eliminates any gray area of impropriety. Sometimes a media outlet will cover the cost of the meal. But a source should never pay for a reporter's meal.

An interview at a meal is a good way to cover several topics at once, get to know a reporter and vice-versa, establish a less formal relationship with the reporter, and save time.

The Pitfalls of E-mail Replies

Reporters will often pose their questions in an e-mail. Should you reply in the email? It depends.

First, remember that e-mails get bounced around. Your reply should be one that you are comfortable with many people reading, including, potentially, your adversaries and your boss.

If the e-mail from a reporter poses a basic question and you are absolutely certain your response is accurate, then it is probably okay to reply in an e-mail. But be very clear and concise. We all have a tendency to be verbose and chatty in e-mails.

If you are unsure whether to hit *send*, imagine your e-mail posted on the front page of a newspaper. Now ask yourself a few questions: Are you comfortable with the content? Are there any inflammatory comments? Will there be any repercussions professionally or personally if your e-mail is viewed by someone other than the intended recipient? Are there any words or phrases that are now making the little hairs on your neck stand up? If so, take them out or hit delete and call the reporter instead.

During a particularly nasty political campaign, a columnist sent a candidate a lengthy e-mail with several detailed questions. In the e-mail reply, the official included some unkind comments about his political opponent and plenty of editorial commentary. The columnist forwarded the entire message to the official's political adversary. The contents were used as part of the adversary's political campaign. Be very careful with e-mails. Only use them as an offensive strategy; i.e., sending press releases and invitations for interviews.

Also, verify that the e-mail is actually from a reporter. If you are unfamiliar with the name or the e-mail address, double-check the authenticity of the message.

Organizing Your Incoming Media Messages:

Set guidelines for how and when you get your messages.

Direct assistants and family members who take the calls to find out the exact topic for discussion and the reporter's deadline and contact numbers.

Designate a single, knowledgeable, trusted spokesperson to speak in your absence.

Instruct all others who take your calls to direct all media inquiries to you or your spokesperson, and never to "chat" with reporters about the topic at hand—or about you.

You and your spokesperson should each have a list of all the reporters' names and the outlets they work for, with their deadlines and contact numbers also noted.

Follow-Up Strategies

It is important to organize and manage follow-up files for all your interviews. This is especially important if you anticipate subsequent stories or a continued relationship with the particular reporter or news outlet.

Don't assume the reporters will keep tabs and follow up on any issue. Keep them apprised of all changes and updates. Call them, send releases, or e-mail them with any new data. It is in your best interest that outdated news isn't repeated or picked up by other news outlets. It's your obligation to "source" all new information.

Make a file of every one of your publicized quotes, plus any notes or bullet points you provided to reporters. Keep copies of all print news in which you are either quoted or referenced. Jot down quotes from radio or television news stories and make note of the airdate. Attach copies of any accompanying reports or written material you provided to reporters during interviews for the story.

You will want to have a record of every one of your quotes. Issues and opinions can change, and there may be a multitude of evolving news pieces and quotes over a long period of time. They will begin to blur in your memory. Re-read your previous quotes on all stories that re-emerge before granting another interview on the subject.

If your position has changed, you can address it before the reporter puts you on the defensive by asking why your comments differ from those you have previously made. Be prepared to offer an effective reply if a reporter says, "Last year you said 'A' and now you are saying 'B.'"

Giving Out Your Personal Information

Be very selective about giving out your cell phone or home phone numbers or private e-mail address to reporters. In some cases, you may want to be accessible at anytime, anywhere. But keep in mind that reporters' deadlines can be at any time of day or night. If they are wrapping up a story at 10 p.m. while an editor impatiently waits for that last detail, they won't hesitate to call you at home to get the information.

Also remember that once you give your personal cell phone number to one reporter at a news outlet, it could be put into a central database. Every reporter and editor who works with that reporter could have access to it. Most reporters would much rather call your personal numbers and avoid dealing with your staff and leaving messages. By calling your cell or your home, they have a much better chance at reaching you directly. And don't rely on caller ID: Every reporter I know is savvy enough to block their numbers when cold-calling sources.

Blown Out of Proportion and Suddenly a News Story

It's the middle of a busy day, you have back-to-back meetings or a big investigation, and you find that you have a half dozen calls from reporters about a topic that, in your opinion, is just an overblown exaggeration, campaign hype, a non-story and, at least to you, a waste of time.

Such stories will crop up once in a while that you might believe have been blown far out of proportion and not worth your time and effort. But never trivialize these matters—they must be important to someone if the media are chasing it down. For the best interest of your image, you should at least take the matter seriously enough to address it.

Rebecca Cooper wrote a column in 2006 about her experience working as a reporter for an award-winning weekly newspaper. She astutely observed that "community activists bristle like spooked terriers if you trivialize their peeves." She's right, and as she also stated in her column, trivializing someone's concern is something you likely will only do once. The memory of your ringing ears and the subsequent fallout will be quite enough to stop you the second time.

Indeed, the blue street sign that was supposed to be green might not seem important to you, but it could be a big deal to someone else. Now, this is not to suggest that you must move heaven and earth to change the color of the sign if it is not necessary, just to quiet a critic. But if your company or department is in the least responsible or involved, then at least get to the bottom of the mistake and apologize when asked about it by a reporter. A little humility, and responsibility, is a good thing for a news source.

No matter the situation, you won't win any fans by trivializing someone else's concerns simply because they don't make much difference to you, or because you think the issue is drivel or hype. When speaking to a reporter, never belittle someone else's genuine concerns and worries no matter how insignificant the matter seems to you.

Step Four:
Understanding Journalists

Journalists, in my opinion, have one of the most interesting and fun, yet stressful, jobs. It's great to work away from a desk, socialize as part of your job, be among the first to know all the news, all the dirt, all the information. There is nothing more exciting than being part of a team of reporters chasing down a big story, trying to get all the information and make deadline.

There are also times a journalist simply wants to hide under a desk, turn off the phone and move swiftly on to another career. Reporters must pry and ask tough questions, often on their source's worst days. It's very difficult to call the fire chief's widow, just hours after her beloved husband died. Or the elected official the morning after he lost the big election. Or the administrator, seeking his reaction on being fired. Try trailing a funeral procession, snapping photos. As a reporter, there are times when you feel more than intrusive, part pariah and part shark. You can't wait to file the story and go home.

For a reporter, it is at once both thrilling and terrifying knowing that thousands, maybe millions, of people are going to read or hear something that you wrote and accept it as fact, as news.

Journalists are always in the know, up on all the latest information. They seem to know everybody and are typically very social creatures. They also work hard, for typically little compensation. They sit with you through a meeting that lasts until midnight. Then you go home and go to sleep. But the reporter works until 3 a.m. so the draft story is filed when their editor wakes at 6 a.m. I have yet to meet a reporter who earns overtime pay.

A journalist also has a unique perspective—on the outside looking in. As a reporter, you watch, you listen, but you almost never participate, always stay on the sidelines. Seasoned reporters become very observant and are good listeners. They develop a keen sense about when someone is lying, and they are usually a good judge of character.

I like to think of good news reporters as announcers at a football game, calling the plays, giving stats and a little background along the way, telling the audience who won and who lost. Bad reporters are more like referees, making judgment calls and influencing the outcome of the game.

As the old adage goes, a reporter is only as good as his or her sources. By better understanding a reporter's job requirements, you will be a better spokesperson and, in turn, you will get better press coverage.

Great Expectations

The news industry is changing fast. In the digital age, reporters must juggle even more stories under shorter deadlines. Most reporters barely have time to verify the information given to them before the story goes onto the website. There are very, very few investigative reporters out there, and certainly small-town papers and radio stations rarely have the luxury of producing investigative pieces. Reporters report what was said, attribute it to a source, and then report what another source said or did.

Some news sources complain that reporters fail to verify some fact or another, or to dig for the details. As a source, if you expect reporters to start doing their own investigations, you will be disappointed. Most don't have the time, the budgets, or the inclination. Would they love to have the absolute truth every time they run a story? Of course. But that is just not how it works. Reporters don't sit as judge and jury; they aren't the referees.

A colleague of mine, a reporter turned spokesperson, once said that if he ever had the chance to offer advice to young reporters, it would be this: "Never become so cynical to ever start a story without seeking the truth, but don't be so naïve as to think you are going to get it."

For example, a reporter is assigned a story outlining speculation about contamination in a community lake. He could quote an environmentalist who suspects that the swimming hole is polluted. Then the reporter might include comments from a biologist who claims the lake does not appear polluted. A good reporter will include confirmation from both sources that no testing of the lake water has been completed. Perhaps the reporter will include a comment from a third source asking why the government hadn't ordered tests before allowing community members to swim or fish in the questionable water. A good photo of children splashing around in the lake would complete the story. But the reporter likely will not collect his or her own sample and send it to a lab to resolve the dispute. That is not a reporter's job.

Tip: Always keep in mind that a reporter's essential job is to report the news. Not to interpret it. Not to influence it. Not to analyze it. And certainly not to protect his or her sources from unflattering coverage.

As a source or spokesperson, keeping your expectations in check will help you better manage your media relations. Don't expect good coverage because a reporter sympathized with you during the interview, because you had dinner with them, because you spent hours preparing and copying all the written material they needed for the story. Don't expect them to ignore your adversaries' side of the issue—even if they acknowledge to you in confidence that they think your opponent is nutty or dishonest. When they are preparing the story, all this fades away, and they deliver all the news—the facts, the conflict, and the color.

Lastly, most seasoned reporters eventually become resigned to the fact that they will make mistakes. They hate it, they still lose sleep over it, but they accept it. Reporters deal with thousands of facts in a typical week. They hear, see, read, and digest massive amounts of information, and then they must turn around and regurgitate it all. Even the best note-takers and observers will make some mistakes.

Reporters Are Not Your Publicists

Just because you pitched a solid news story with an enticing angle doesn't mean you will get the coverage you desire every time. But if you are prepared, and educated, you can creatively influence coverage surrounding you or your cause.

You can't dictate exactly what will appear in the news. If you try to overtly manipulate the story or push it too hard, any editors or reporters worth their salt will intentionally take the story a different way. They might leave you out, drop the story, or investigate every comment you make with the precision of a forensic technician intent on finding a contradiction. This sends you a message that they are not your publicists.

Reporters work with little or no obligation to their sources. They may negotiate with you, develop an amiable rapport, and collaborate with you. But the story is their master. Yes, there is a mutual need between reporter and source, but the minute you begin to think that the media are obligated to promote you or your agenda, you start sliding down a slippery slope.

At one time, the media's role sometimes slipped into a gray area. Reporters helped keep Franklin D. Roosevelt's illness and John Kennedy's dalliances from the public. Some news was quashed under a gentlemen's agreement among journalists that withholding the information was for the greater good. These days, with rare exception, this gray area has mostly vanished. And this change in attitude toward transparency is, for the most part, a good thing.

As a New York City police officer in the 1950s and 1960s, my father would tell tales of law enforcement collaborating with reporters to ferret out criminals. They had standard tactics that, he said, were often very successful.

For instance, if police had a hunch that a suspect was hiding out with a friend or relative somewhere in the city, they might ask the media to announce that they believed the suspect had fled to the West Coast, and that law enforcement there had taken over the search. Or they might ask reporters to say that the focus had shifted to another suspect. The news would come out; the suspect would get a false sense of security and come out of hiding. The police, of course, would then monitor potential hideouts, and when their guy emerged, they would nab him. Another tactic was to "leak" that they planned to raid several suspected hideouts the following morning. In anticipation of the raid, antsy criminals would flee from their shelter, right into the arms of police.

But, of course, the journalism business has changed over the past 50 or 60 years. For the most part, every issue, every item deemed newsworthy is fair game. Journalists do not report or fail to report depending on how it impacts sources.

Never fall into a sense of security that a reporter will hold information that sheds a negative light on you. Reporters are not there for you. Ever. They are there to provide information to the public.

Tip: How you present the news to reporters is almost as important as the content itself.

Generally, reporters are skeptical of public relations representatives. They refer to PR reps as "flacks" (the word seems to be a combination of "flattery" and "hack") and roll their eyes at the blatant spin. They don't want to be sold on a story. They don't want to give away free publicity that is better suited to a paid advertisement. Reporters want a news hook, and then they want a story to develop around it. If you push a story too hard, an editor may drop it. If you have your PR puppet call every time you make contact with them, the reporter will eventually begin to ignore you. An experienced PR agent can be a big asset, but there must be a balance.

Most of the revenue generated in the news industry comes from advertisements, not subscriptions. There is a fine line between news and ads, especially in small communities. A new business opening its doors might be newsworthy. A business moving locations or sponsoring a charitable event is sometimes newsworthy. But business owners sometimes seek press coverage on whatever it is they offer their customers: a new product, reduced prices, an expanded showroom. That information belongs in an ad.

Candidates for office often make the same mistake by holding press conferences whenever they have a new idea or each time an opponent fires off criticism. Many reporters don't have time, or inclination, to attend numerous press conferences announcing minor details or promotional material. It is best to save the news conferences for the big-ticket items.

Because the world of media is a business, most editors and publishers are very wary of giving away free publicity. This is where the news hook and the angle come into play again. By pitching a fresh angle or tying your story into a growing trend, a holiday, or an event, you have a better chance of winning coverage.

When Dealing With A Reporter, Never:

Offer to exchange goods or services for a fluff piece on your campaign or business.

Promise a hot tip about someone else in exchange for a fluff piece about you or your business.

Ask to see, or demand to approve, the story before it goes to print.

Ask for their opinion on the issue being discussed.

Berate a reporter for not giving you prominent placement or using your "good" quotes.

Hold a press conference intended solely to criticize an opponent or competitor.

A Reporter's Perspective

Despite the angle of the story, despite your perspective on the news being delivered, and no matter if you are fielding accolades, promoting a new business, or squirming in the hot seat, it is important to remember that the reporter's perspective remains constant.

Remember, a reporter's investment in the story isn't nearly as big as yours. Keep your expectations about the upcoming story in check. They likely will never produce the news piece exactly the same way you would. It is prepared from a much more objective—and less invested—stance.

The reporter's position—on the outside, looking in—remains the same whether you are on the offensive or on the defensive. They need to fill in the same blanks, construct the building blocks of the story by learning the "Who, What, When, Where, and Why," with as many absolutes as possible. So while the nuances of the interview might change depending on the slant and on the source's position, the context, the basic tenets of dealing with the media do not change with the angle of the story. An effective news source follows the same basic guidelines in every circumstance.

Reporters are just doing their jobs. Your best strategy is to deal with them in the same way you would deal with any colleague or client.

This means telling the truth and sticking to main message points. It's easy to embellish when we are on the defensive, or when we are enthusiastic about our cause. A good journalist will always pick up on inconsistencies. Reporters typically interview more than one person for a story, or they may have spoken to you previously on the topic under discussion. You could end up with unflattering coverage if your responses don't jibe with other sources or with your previous comments.

Stay even-keeled. Never get defensive or overly enthusiastic. A hard sell could alienate reporters or prompt them to poke around at secondary issues. Reporters are doing their job. To maintain a productive relationship with a reporter, keep the conversation amiable.

Editorials

There is often confusion about the distinction between news stories and editorials or commentary. Editorials are opinion pieces, based on fact, and written by an editor; commentary is provided by a staff member or sometimes a columnist paid by the news outlet. Editorials and commentary are usually placed in a designated section of the paper and clearly marked as opinion pieces.

If my experience is any indication, reporters take a lot of unfair heat from their sources over editorials. If you have an issue with an editorial, bring it to the attention of the editors or publishers. Taking out your frustration over an unflattering editorial on a reporter is unfair and unproductive. The reporter likely didn't write the opinion piece, probably has no control over what appears on the editorial pages, and possible doesn't even agree with the opinions within the editorial.

Tip: Never lambast a reporter over an editorial written by his or her boss.

I always advise news sources never to take editorials too seriously. They are, after all, just opinions. If you strongly disagree with the content, write a letter for publication expressing your opposing views. Some papers have guest editorial columns, which offer more space and allow for a longer written reply.

If, however, the editorial contains factual errors, you should contact both the reporter and the editor. Do this when you are calm, not upset. Point out the mistakes and request a correction. Write your own letter and advise the readers of the errors. If the opinions were aired on a television or radio broadcast, contact the producers. Send e-mails or call clients, constituents, or stakeholders who could be upset or confused over the editorial and the factual errors.

Editors sometimes use the opinions section to generate discussion. They may not agree 100 percent with the opinions they offer. Instead, they are publishing a controversial stance to get people talking about the issue and about themselves and their news outlet. (Remember, news is a business.) Getting readers or an audience to mention the editorial or a particular column around the dinner table or during discussions over a controversial issue is sometimes an editor's goal.

In most cases, however, the editorials represent a newspaper's, television station's or web news site's official position on politics, an event or some public controversy.

If you disagree with an editorial, offer your own position in the form of a letter or column. Leave the reporter alone, and don't take any personal shots at the editor for simply offering his own views. Publicly trashing the media rarely gets you any points. The best tack for any news source is disagreeing while remaining civil and courteous.

> **When Writing A Letter to the Editor:**
>
> *Keep it brief; a few succinct paragraphs.*
>
> *Stay on point.*
>
> *If critical, refer to the story or editorial, not the journalist.*
>
> *Don't get pulled into a back-and-forth letter-writing war; write just one letter.*
>
> *Many papers don't accept letters simultaneously submitted to other publications; check the paper's policy.*

Dealing with Reporters Who Are Less Than Professional

I think most reporters are professional, well informed, and do a good job of getting the pertinent facts out in a fair and honest way. But, as in any profession, there are inferior reporters, and if you deal with journalists enough, you are bound to run across a few.

In my experience as both a news reporter and a spokesperson, the few reporters who I believed did a poor job were mostly just inexperienced—right out of college, early 20s, first time they dealt professionally with lawyers, police officers, elected officials, business owners. When I began reporting, I had a long learning curve myself. It's the nature of the business.

Some young reporters have a difficult time interacting with sources who are closer to their parents' age than their own. They may clam up and get nervous, be virtually unable to ask the tough questions, or overcompensate and attack with rapid-fire questions. Others haven't yet grasped the necessary organizational skills that go along with being a good reporter. As a news source you must be prepared to deal with all types of reporters—experienced and inexperienced both—and still get the best media coverage possible.

If all the following tips do not work and you have trouble with a particular reporter, talk to his or her editor. Expect the editor to be defensive ... most protect their young cub reporters with a fierceness that may catch you off guard. Don't attack the reporter personally. Simply explain in detail why the coverage was inaccurate or inadequate.

As a last resort, tape the interviews yourself, or ask that all questions be submitted in writing. These tactics are not popular with editors or reporters, but if you have an ongoing problem with one particular reporter, you can cover yourself by keeping a taped or e-mail record of their exact questions and your exact responses.

How To Deal With Reporters Who:

Are perpetually unprepared: This can be an irritating problem for any news source. Good reporters do their homework before they call you and should have most of the background. I recall one reporter who constantly lost paperwork we provided to her—we began keeping extra copies in our office, anticipating her visit for a second round of reports, releases, agendas. I began sending her as many files as I could via e-mail, so that if she lost something, she could access it and re-print it from her own computer.

There is little to be done in these cases: you will likely repeat a lot of information and make a good number of extra copies. Sending information to the editor can work sometimes, but editors have enough paperwork piled on their desks, and most won't appreciate getting more.

Pepper you with rapid-fire questions: This can be a nervous habit for some reporters; others are just antsy and aren't really listening to the replies—their thoughts are always on the next question. They interrupt you, switch topics while you are in mid-sentence, fire off six questions before you even sit down for the interview.

Try not to become unnerved when peppered with questions— particularly if you're on camera or with a group of other people. Wait a few seconds, collect your thoughts, and then say, "There are a good number of questions being asked all at once, so let's take them one at a time so I can respond fully and you can report it accurately." Then address each question individually. If the reporter interrupts again, just say you will get to the next question, but you would like the opportunity to finish your thoughts on the previous question.

Use you as a general information resource: I had a reporter call me once to ask me for the office phone number for a state senator for whom I did not work—in fact, one whom I had never met, and whose office was 50 miles west of mine.

Providing information relative to your position is a must in most cases. But don't allow yourself to become a general reference source for overworked or lazy reporters. Beware those who repeatedly call you for information they could—and should—be researching on their own. This is actually a very common problem. It's a tricky balance. As a news source you want to be helpful. But don't fall into the trap of doing reporters' jobs for them.

As spokesperson, when new reporters started, I always took the time to provide them with a list of all the staff they would deal with, along with contact numbers and correct titles. I told them which offices could provide which information, and even gave them tips on how to track down some public data that could be tricky to find. Make a small file with all the pertinent, basic information about your office, department or business, and give it to each reporter you deal with. Make sure to update it regularly—don't expect them to change the title of a staff member who was promoted—do it yourself. Date each file so they can keep track of the most recent, and send off the updated information every couple of months.

Reporters who call just before deadline: If a reporter repeatedly contacts you just minutes prior to their deadline, giving you little or no time to reply or research an answer, call the reporter when he or she is not on deadline and discuss this problem. Explain that you need ample time to prepare and to help get the information they need. Set a timeline that works for both of you. Address this issue first with the reporter. If the last-minute calls continue, contact the editor.

Sometimes, when dealing with a sensitive or big story, a reporter will intentionally contact sources at the last minute. They want to spring the story on the source to get a genuine, spontaneous reaction. Or two reporters will call two different sources at exactly the same time and ask identical questions. Then they compare responses. They sometimes call at the last minute so one source does not have time to confer with other sources or to give someone else the heads-up that the reporter will be calling.

But this is a rare situation. If a reporter is constantly calling you right before deadline, work it out with the reporter and his or her editor. The reporter should be giving you plenty of time to respond.

Biased reporters: Reporters are human—they develop biases and opinions just like everyone else. Many journalists live in the communities they cover, so it is natural that they will form opinions on the news and on their sources. As stated earlier, like in any profession, there are good and bad journalists. The good ones keep their bias to a minimum with the context of their stories. The not-so-good ones use their stories as an instrument to promote one side or take down another. Eventually, ethical editors and producers will remove those reporters from a story or a beat.

If you feel you have evidence that a reporter appears to have a bias that colors his or her coverage, the first step is to set up a face-to-face-meeting with the editor. But you'd better have a good deal of solid evidence to support your case. One or two questionable stories is not enough. An accusation of bias is a serious one in the world of journalism, so if you decide to press the issue, be prepared.

Depending on the response of the editor, you can ask him or her to assign another reporter. Mostly, you will have to work around this problem, as is it not easily solved. If there are other reporters covering the same issues for competing news outlets, the disparity between the biased reporter's stories and the others' stories will eventually reveal the slanted coverage.

Reporters who put words in your mouth: There may be times when, following your comment, a reporter will suggest that you "say it this way" so the quote will be shorter, make a catchy sound bite or just fit better into the context of the story. This is more likely to occur with on-air interviews—either on the radio or for TV news.

Always be careful in this situation—don't let anyone put words in your mouth; one word can twist the meaning or the tone of your entire message.

Deliver your own message and stay focused. And beware the reporter who urges you to "just have fun with it." You don't want to relax to the point where you say something you didn't intend to say.

Help Them Help You Get Better Coverage

What elements are necessary for a complete news story? Mostly the answers to the 5 W's: *Who is it about? What is it about? When did, or will, it happen? Where is the story centered? Why did this story happen?* And sometimes *How did this get to this point, and/or how will this affect the community?*

In most circumstances, reporters will also ask: What happens next? Reporters like timelines. They will want you to quantify when possible. They will need colorful quotes. They will get reaction to the story from supporters and opponents both.

To flesh out a complete story, reporters will need background materials and any related documentation. If you make an attempt to anticipate these questions and prepare copies of reports, documents, charts and agendas before the interview, it will help the reporter meet deadline and produce an accurate story. If you e-mail a reporter the link to a 200-page report, don't expect him or her to read it all the way through. Time constraints may prohibit a reporter from doing so. Directing the reporter to the most pertinent information within the report helps deliver the news effectively.

Some sources provide condensed reports for the media, reducing a 100-page document down to a 10-page summation. Some reporters won't like this idea and will assume you have censored the material to your benefit. It's a better idea to give them the entire document with pertinent facts highlighted. For instance, if you are providing a journalist a copy of a lengthy court decision or a budget, go through the document, whether it is electronic or on paper, and highlight or bold the main points and summations. This is especially important with legal documents.

Keep their deadlines in mind; don't schedule a press conference or an important meeting an hour before deadline.

Save seats for reporters, photographers and television cameras in the front row at meetings, public hearings, and press conferences.

Another way to help a reporter is to keep your comments brief. Long prepared statements are both confusing and boring. If you do make a lengthy speech, give a written copy to journalists following your presentation.

Every news source benefits from accurate reporting and educated journalists. By organizing background and supporting materials for journalists, you are helping them deliver more complete stories. When or your business or campaign are the subject of that story, you should do everything you can to help them.

Whether you are on the offensive or defensive with a reporter, follow these basic guidelines in every interview, no matter the circumstance:

Be honest, never exaggerate; drop the hyperbole.

Convey, and repeat, your main message points.

Be enthusiastic, but don't oversell the story.

Be good-humored.

Provide all the necessary background material.

Don't trivialize others' concerns and interests.

Step Five:
Why Did They Burn Me?

There is typically a disparity between the mindset of a source and that of a reporter. This difference in philosophy can create major tension when one side doesn't understand the other.

A reporter can often become *persona non grata* after covering the same beat for a lengthy amount of time. Familiarity, as they say, can breed contempt. Sometimes, this is because they have hurt sources with inaccurate reporting or bias. Or because there is a perception that they have been unfair, warranted or not. But more likely it is simply because a source at some point developed a fondness or connection to the reporter, let his or her guard down, forgot the journalist's goals and professional obligations, and then at some point felt betrayed.

But the bottom line is that reporters are not your friends, and they are not your enemies. They are just doing their job. So if you feel you have been treated unfairly, take a close, objective look at the coverage. Then pick your battles carefully.

Were You *Really* Burned? Philosophical Differences

Your goal as a source is to get your story out to the public, promote your cause, or explain your side of an issue. The reporters' job is to provide a much broader picture that will include other perspectives along with yours. Sometimes when a source imagines a story one way but it comes out quite differently, he or she feels burned. As a source, you may not be the best judge of coverage that highlights you or your cause. A news source's perspective and philosophy is very different from that of a journalist.

Famed White House press corps reporter Helen Thomas once revealed during an interview that she sometimes asked questions intended to bring a source, especially an elected official, "down in size." And perhaps this type of commentary adds to a source's trepidation when dealing with the media: the fear that they will be mistreated.

The majority of reporters are not out to get you, and they do attempt to get the story right. A school official told me once that he completely ignores all reporters because "they never get it right." And, indeed, it is frustrating to see misinformation in the news. But when a source complains that reporters "never get it right," then it is time they begin taking a close look at 1) how they are presenting the information, and 2) how they are interpreting the final versions of the stories.

There are specific ways to counter errors, misquotes and poor coverage. But first determine if you have really been burned and whether you are better served by complaining or just letting it go.

Pick Your Battles

The first thing to do if you feel a story about you or your cause is unfair or in error is to show it to a trusted colleague or friend and ask for an honest appraisal. Choose someone who can be objective about the content.

Remember, you may not be the best judge of whether coverage is fair. No matter how the final version of a news story is produced, it is very likely that is will never be exactly how you would have delivered the news yourself. Your judgment could be clouded by emotion and subjectivity. A neutral opinion will help you better assess the story.

- If your advisors agree that there are some problems with the story, consider the specifics of the errors, make a list, and then assess exactly why you are upset:

- If you are unhappy because your competitor's comments were placed at the beginning of the story and yours were at the end, forget about making a complaint to the reporter or editor. They are entitled to make judgment calls about the placement of details within a news piece, and they're not likely to be receptive to criticism on the subject.

- You won a huge case or completed a massive project. You are thrilled. The media calls, and you gladly give them an interview. Then the story comes out, and the slant of the article is critical. In this case, again, you don't have much leverage to complain. Remember that winning in court or completing your personal agenda does not necessarily entitle you to positive coverage. Public support and media support don't always automatically follow the victor. And if you gloat or pound your chest too much following a personal victory, you might actually encourage more critical coverage. A little humility goes a long way in helping you get better coverage in the wake of a big personal accomplishment.

- The story doesn't include all the details you provided. In this case, complaints may or may not be justified. Reporters can't possibly include every fact and quote they collect in a story. List the details that were left out. If these omissions drastically change the tone or angle of the story, then consider contacting the reporter or editor. But in these cases, don't sweat the small stuff. Pick your battles.

- If your comments were left out completely and you play a vital role in the story, then write a letter to the editor for publication offering your comments on the issue. You can also contact the reporter to ask why all your input was omitted—but, again, in most cases this is a judgment call on their part and they are entitled to make these kinds of decisions. If the story is about you or your cause and the only comments used are criticism from your opponents, then you have the right to complain. You should have the opportunity to defend accusations within the story.

- If your name, position, title, or company is spelled wrong, or if the story included inaccurate statistics then it is time to seek a correction. *Ask* for one. Do not *demand* one. In my experience, editors don't respond well to someone barking orders at them.

Decide whether they *really* burned you and then determine how best to handle it. Ignore the small stuff and the judgment calls made by the editors (e.g., placement of your quotes). Bring attention to misspellings and other minor errors so they are not repeated later. Ask for corrections or clarifications for larger errors (dates, statistics, etc.).

Quoted Out of Context or Misquoted: Seeking Corrections

Complaints that someone was quoted out of context or misquoted are common. They are also the most difficult to prove. Sometimes, when a reporter paraphrases your comments or shortens your quotes, the meaning becomes skewed. Your best bet here is prevention—asking that your quotes be read back to you and speaking in brief sentences, offering just short quotes that are on point.

When a quote is reported that is drastically off base and inaccurate, seek a clarification. Call the reporter and the editor and calmly explain that the news story did not accurately illustrate what you discussed with the reporter. Since this falls within the boundaries of a miscommunication rather than a mistake on the reporter's part, its best to seek a *clarification* instead of a correction. The editor or producer might put together a short news article—a sentence or two—clarifying your comments.

Clear up your comments in a letter to the editor. Do not criticize the reporter, just refer to the inaccuracies in the news article. Briefly re-state your initial comments to the reporter. If the misquotes could have been read by a client, supporter, your boss or colleagues, send them a copy of the letter to the editor with a brief note explaining the problem. Try to do this as quickly as possible after the misquote is published.

When writing a letter to the editor, keep it brief and on point. If someone counters your comments with their own letters, do not be drawn into a back-and-forth letter war. Write just a single letter stating your views.

Attach the correction or clarification to the original article and keep it in a file with all your media coverage. Review all subsequent stories on the issue to make sure the mistake isn't repeated. To save time, many print reporters "cut and paste" background paragraphs from earlier stories on the same topic into new stories. Cutting and pasting is a bad habit that can lead to outdated or erroneous information being repeated.

Never ask a reporter from a competing news outlet to report on an error made by a rival. Despite fierce competition between news outlets, most reporters tend to have a pretty high level of professional courtesy and will probably refuse anyway. You can, however, bring attention to the error in the first news piece so that it is not picked up and used in other stories, in other outlets.

Defending yourself as "misquoted" frequently could damage your credibility. Being misquoted or having comments taken out of context will happen once in a while. It's simply conversational miscommunication or misinterpretation. If it happens repeatedly, take a good hard look at how you are handling your interviews. Try to determine why you are being misinterpreted.

Are you making brief concise message points in order or importance? Or are you rambling on and on and on?

Are you providing all the necessary written material and background information? Or are you relying on the reporter to get all the ancillary materials on his or her own?

Are you focusing on the interview, really listening to the questions? Or are you conducting the interview on a cell phone while signing paperwork and sorting through your mail?

To correct a mistake:

Call the reporter and editor to advise them of the error.

Do not address the error when you are upset or angry.

Provide backup material with the accurate facts.

When misquoted, seek a clarification of what you said.

Write a letter to the editor correcting the story.

When Another Source Provides Inaccurate Information

Publicly correcting another source is always tricky and must be handled very tactfully. If a news report about you or your business includes inaccurate information attributed to another source, how do you handle it?

This depends on who the other source is. Is it friend or foe? If the bad info came from someone in your camp, bring it to his or her attention and ask that person to contact the reporter. They should apologize to the reporter, offer the correct information, and then write a letter to the editor or producer explaining the situation. If the reported information has the potential of misleading clients, constituents or supporters, ask the source to reach out to them also to correct the errors.

If you do not know the source who provided the misinformation, you must take a different approach. First, double-check the facts and make sure it's not *you* who is mistaken about the information. Once you are certain that the facts attributed to the other source are inaccurate, call the reporter and discuss your concerns. Offer to provide them with the supporting material to prove that your facts are the correct ones.

In this type of situation, you always risk offending the other source who might feel angry or embarrassed that you called attention to his or her error. To avoid this, discuss your concerns about offending the other source with the reporter. Ask them to look into the matter without mentioning your name. If you feel comfortable doing so, you can contact the other source and tactfully mention that you suspect the information is inaccurate. Then let them take the lead from there.

If a situation arises in which you hadn't noticed the misinformation yourself, but it is brought to your attention by a reporter who is asking you to go on the record to correct it, be as tactful as possible. Correcting someone else's mistake publicly can be tricky, and if it isn't done with care, you will end up looking bad. Simply state the accurate facts and leave it at that.

If an opponent or adversary intentionally provides misleading information about you to the media, take a more defensive tactic and submit a strongly worded correction in the form of a letter to the editor or seek a televised interview. The focus of the comeback must be correcting the information. Criticizing your opponent for providing it should be a secondary element, if included at all.

Avoid criticizing the reporter for not verifying the information before reporting it as news. Just correct the misinformation, mention that it came from your adversary and let it go at that. If you fear this bad information will spread, make sure all the journalists covering your cause or business are aware that the information is in error even if they didn't report it. You don't want the misinformation picked up by other news outlets and reported as fact.

Step Six:
On Camera Interviews and Photographs

Interviews on camera provide the opportunity to present yourself to the audience in your own unique way. Televised appearances give you the chance to make a visual impression and afford you a stronger connection to your constituents, supporters, clients, or stakeholders. You become more than just a name and a title.

As a news source, you'll need to make your best impression during those 90 seconds of airtime or in that 3x5 photo on the front page.

Handling Televised Interviews

If you haven't spoken on camera before—or even if you have—you will likely be nervous. It's natural to get the jitters when a television camera lens is focused on you. Your best antidote is to be prepared. Even if you are familiar with the topic, take time to anticipate the questions and rehearse your responses. Ask a colleague or family member to toss out some questions and see if you can answer them succinctly and accurately. Ask yourself the ten questions from Step One.

Tip: Always rehearse before a television interview: ask a colleague familiar with the topic to ask you anticipated questions.

Memorize your message points. Practice brief, focused statements. Remind yourself to smile and look at the reporter, not into the camera. Do not glance back and forth between the camera and the reporter. Before the interview, always have a sip of water to keep your voice clear and to prevent dry mouth, coughing, and, spittle.

Before an on camera interview, the reporter may suggest a pre-interview. This is a good opportunity to get a handle on the specific questions that will be asked and to prepare your concise responses. Keep your answers short and to the point. Television segments are brief and your interview may be whittled down to 5 or 10 seconds. Long replies will be edited and the abbreviated version could fail to accurately convey your message.

Televised interviews are either live or taped. Many sources become more nervous about live interviews, fearful they will choke up or that the reporter will stump them with an unexpected question. But live interviews are actually a better opportunity for most news sources to present themselves and their positions on their own terms.

Tip: Live interviews give you the advantage because your comments will not be edited and because the audience hears the reporter's questions along with your responses.

Nothing is taken out of context in a live interview. Also, the reporter must consider his or her own image on camera and must be cognizant of the time frame allotted for the discussion. They will want to keep the interview tight and focused. This means they will typically spend more time preparing with you during a pre-interview.

Of course, during a live interview you do indeed risk being thrown a curve ball, asked a question intended to catch you off-guard. But if you are prepared with your memorized message points, you can ignore the controversial context within the question and swing your reply back to one of your message points. You do this by answering with *"Well, that is another story but the main issue to remember here is….."* or *"The focus here should be…."* Keep your answers positive and reflective of your primary position.

And lastly, never read from a prepared statement during a live interview. Memorize your comments.

Your Image on Screen

A source's image on camera, whether on television or in a still photo, is an important aspect of any interview. How you dress, how you speak, and your mannerisms all create an impression that can influence the audience's interpretation of your comments.

When scheduling a news interview, always be prepare for a photographer or a television camera. Even some print reporters these days carry their own video cameras. The interviews are then aired on the papers' web sites. And many reporters, especially at smaller-circulation newspapers, take their own photos to accompany their stories.

Wardrobe:

Plan your wardrobe carefully. Do you want to convey a casual image? A professional one? What is the event or issue? You might not want to wear a suit when discussing new plans for a Little League field. Instead, dress casually and schedule the interview near the site of the new park or in an existing park. When delivering news about a crisis event, you may want a more polished, authoritative image—a suit and tie or a uniform.

When in doubt, a solid-colored blazer and collared shirt works well for both men and women. Keep a spare blazer at your office or in your car in case of an unexpected interview.

Choose solid-colored clothing for televised interviews and photographs. Patterns can take on an odd, exaggerated appearance on camera. Wide stripes, houndstooth, or a tie with a busy pattern do not play well on camera. Also, avoid bright white shirts and super-bright or neon colors. Bold colors are fine—and sometimes even encouraged for still photographs—but don't select anything overly bright or flashy.

If you have fair skin, avoid red. On camera, your skin could appear very pale and colorless. Whatever your skin tone, select a color that contrasts a bit with your natural coloring. Do not wear a blouse, shirt, jacket, or scarf in a color very close to your skin tone—a tan blouse can wash-out a tan complexion on screen.

No matter what you choose to wear, make sure it is wrinkle-free and clean. Take off hats with brims—they will cast a shadow on your face. Remove your sunglasses unless the glare is so strong that you are squinting without them.

Appearance:

When seated for an on camera interview or for a photograph, pull down the back of your jacket and sit on it. Keep your hands folded in your lap. Don't slouch and avoid crossing and uncrossing your legs. Sit straight, cross your legs, and place your hands on your top leg. Don't lean all the way back into the chair. Sit up, slightly away from the back of the chair. If you are seated at a table, don't rest your chin in your hand or lean your elbows on the table.

If you are standing, never lean against a wall or door jam. For men, one trick to appearing relaxed is to put one hand in the pocket of your pants. Lawyers sometimes put both hands in their front pockets as they address a judge or jury to give the appearance of being completely relaxed and self-assured.

If you are speaking at a podium, bring talking points and place them before you on the podium. Place your hands on the podium. Do not read from a prepared statement. Glance down at your bullet points to remind yourself of the flow of your comments. Focus on whomever you are addressing, not the camera. If photographers are in the room, gesture with one hand once in awhile so they can take a photo that includes some minimal action or movement. Editors typically do not care for photos of speakers at a podium but they will sometimes use them if there is some movement in the photo—the subject points to a map, pushes their glasses up on their nose, points to another person in the room.

Speaking on Camera:

Once you have memorized your talking points and you feel prepared for the questions, it is time for your presentation.

Before the camera is set up, have a sip of water and get rid of the mint or gum in your mouth.

Speak slowly and avoid using slang or acronyms. Remember to ditch the technical jargon. Do not get defensive. Stay good-humored, stay calm, and be direct no matter what the topic of discussion.

If a reporter interrupts you on camera wrap up your comment quickly so you are not speaking over the next question. If you are among several people simultaneously interviewed, wait for a question to be posed directly to you. Refrain from interrupting another source or piggybacking comments onto their statements. When being interviewed on camera as part of a group, always ask the reporter for a pre-interview.

> Consider This: Rhetorical Questions
>
> Never ask a rhetorical question during an on-camera interview. If the interview is edited, you could appear to be asking an actual question.
>
> A candidate for federal office asked rhetorically during a televised interview, "What does this job entail?" and then proceeded to describe all the duties of the office she was seeking.
>
> When the interview was replayed during a subsequent news segment, the rhetorical question aired but the remainder of the interview was edited out. As a result, the candidate appeared to be asking, "What does this job entail?" as if she had no idea what to expect if she won the election. Viewers who hadn't seen the original interview in its entirety would have assumed that she was indeed seeking that answer instead of posing the question in the rhetorical.

News Photographs

If you have scheduled an event and news photographers attend, make sure you reserve some space for them. Photographers will need a clear shot of any action so the designated area should be near the front, off to the side. Ask the photographers specifically who and what they will be shooting.

There are a few tricks to looking better in photographs:

- Tilt your head slightly up and blink when the photographer asks if you are ready, just before they take the shot, so you wont blink when the shutter clicks.

- If you are holding a document, proclamation, or any other prop, hold it in front of your waist or just slightly to the side.

- If the sun or a glare is causing you to squint, advise the photographer and ask that the setting be shifted a bit. Remember to take off any hats with a brim as it could cast a shadow across your face.

Finally, be aware of who is being photographed with you. A news source trying to present a positive image does not want to be standing in a photo with someone with a questionable lifestyle or criminal history. I recall an instance when a public official at a fundraiser was asked by a reporter to pose for a group photo. The official summoned over his staff members, one of whom invited a friend to join in. That *friend* turned out to have a long criminal history and was well known in the community. The politician was fortunate that the photo never appeared in the local news. If it had, his constituents may have been left wondering why he was associating with a criminal element when in fact he did not know this individual at all.

Tip: If you are posing for a photograph and are hoping the picture lands on the newspaper's front page, wear a brightly colored shirt (solid not print). Editors of newspapers with color front pages like bright photos that capture attention. They won't likely choose a photo of people wearing black, white or grey.

The Live Mike

Once your interview has concluded, say *nothing* other than to offer a brief thank you to the reporter. The microphone may appear to be turned off and the cameraperson may appear to be finished shooting. But audio equipment and cameras can remain "live' for several minutes. Your voice and image may continue to be taped or picked up on the live feed long after the interview concludes.

There have been countless sources caught on a live mike or camera saying or doing something that overshadowed the actual story. Even seasoned reporters and anchors have gotten themselves in trouble by unwittingly speaking into a live mike.

Televised Interviews:

Be prepared with your comments—don't wing it.

Look at the reporter, not the television camera.

Speak in short, declarative sentences.

Wear solid colors; avoid busy patterns.

Never ask a rhetorical question on camera.

Remain silent after the interview until you're certain the microphone is off.

Step Seven:
Pitching Your Story: Publicity Tips

In most cases, the angle of the news emerges as the reporter begins to build the story. The pendulum can swing either way. If given the option of a positive slant or a negative one, the latter usually wins with journalists unless a creative angle is introduced for the positive story.

The status quo is boring. Good news? Not always interesting. It is no surprise that negative stories generally generate more interest.

But there is another element to all of this: sources looking for better press coverage must consider the following---the credo that people shouldn't get extra credit simply for doing what they are *supposed* to do. This is vital because this philosophy rings true with most journalists.

Maybe journalist's expectations are higher. Maybe they tend to be a bit idealistic. Either way, successfully completing a task that you are *expected* to complete typically won't earn you much kudos in the media.

Consider this example: Two government bodies within the same news coverage area received annual bond credit ratings from Standard and Poor's and Moody's. One was awarded stellar ratings, the highest ever awarded in that region. The other district's rating dropped one point below the previous year. The latter landed on the front page. The high rating was barely mentioned.

The officials who received the elevated rating were upset. They had campaigned on fiscal responsibility. They promised to produce tight budgets, spend taxpayer money wisely, and keep debt in check. And they did. So why wasn't there more coverage of their accomplishments? Because there was no conflict, there was no change, and there was no big story. They did what was expected of them.

But the negative story represented a decline, a fiscal failure that could cost taxpayer's money. Those officials reacted appropriately with a mea culpa and promises to improve. Then they scheduled a series of public meetings to discuss the municipality's finances.

So, how could the officials who received the top rating have generated more coverage on their achievement? They could have shifted the angle of the story. Instead of doling out a bland press release about a bond rating, they could have pitched a peripheral story with an interesting news hook relative to the rating.

For example, the elevated credit rating resulted in lower interest rates, saving the municipality hundreds of thousands of dollars. A portion of that money was allocated for an adult day care program. For several hours each week, nurses provide respite for caregivers of patients with Alzheimer's and other serious ailments. Inviting the reporter to the day care center to interview the caregivers (typically spouses) about how this program improved their quality of life might have garnered press coverage relative to the bond rating. A human-interest story about this valuable program would have highlighted the tangible byproducts of the officials' elevated fiscal rating.

Reporters don't want to miss a positive story. They want to report on a variety of news, positive and negative, but if they feel they are getting the hard sell, or that the news is stale or boring, they will pass. And as busy as they are, focused on myriad stories each week, they may not always connect all the dots on their own. It is up to the savvy news source to pitch the fresh angles.

Tip: Timing, the story angle, and the way you pitch the idea could determine whether you get good press coverage or no coverage at all.

Be sure to consider the news outlet that best fits the tone of your story. If you have a fast-paced story with plenty of visuals—a unique setting or a jam-packed protest—then television is a good option for coverage. Remember that television reporters rarely cover events that have already occurred—protests, meetings, press conferences. They want to be at the scene.

More complicated issues, ongoing stories with a narrow focus or complicated history, and events that have past are often more suitable for print news and web news sites. Details of a comprehensive story can often be conveyed more fully in a newspaper or magazine article than in a brief televised segment.

Time-sensitive announcements intended to reach as many people as possible in the shortest amount of time are best placed in radio spots, in mass emails, on web news sites, and on blogs and podcasts. If time permits, daily newspapers can be useful too.

Be selective about which reporter to contact. A journalist with a business beat doesn't want to hear a pitch about a new environmental research plan; the crime reporter doesn't want to hear about the new housing development; and the arts editor won't likely cover a political campaign. If you are unfamiliar with the reporters, research their previous stories and find someone who routinely covers themes similar to the story you plan to pitch.

Think about your story idea and ask yourself some questions: Why is it unique and newsworthy? Where are the conflict, change and color? What would make this interesting to the average media audience? Apply the "*so what?*" test.

If you are pitching a story to a reporter you do not know:

- *Identify who you are and why you are calling.*

- *Ask if this is a good time to discuss your idea. If it isn't, ask the reporter to suggest the best time to call back.*

- *Let the reporter know you are familiar with their publication and stories.*

- *Briefly explain the idea and why the audience will be interested.*

- *Ask the reporter if they would like to meet for an interview.*

Timing is Everything

Timing is truly everything with regard to media relations.

When you pitch a story and *how long* you take to present the material are important elements to consider when seeking press coverage.

First, learn the deadlines of all the reporters you deal with. Don't assume all are the same, or even close. Reporters for daily newspapers may have an afternoon deadline each weekday; don't pitch a brand new story idea to them at 2 p.m. Contact them early in the morning. Reporters for weeklies will typically have a specific day and time each week by which they must have all their material submitted to the editor. Pitch stories to reporters at weekly publications on the day the newspaper hits the stands—that is when they are most likely considering stories for the next week's edition.

Radio and television stations set deadlines based on the time their news programs air. Call them well in advance, preferably in the morning, to provide ample time to get reporters and cameras to the location. Monthly publications—magazines and newsletters—are often prepared weeks or months in advance. Don't want until June to pitch a story idea related to Fourth of July celebrations.

Tip: When in doubt about deadlines, call or send your release in the early morning on a Monday or Tuesday.

Consider the reporter's deadline as *your* deadline. Don't call them an hour before their deadline to give them a story tip. Knowing they wont have time to work on the story, they may pass completely.

Another element to timing is discerning whether it's a busy news week or a slow one. Pitch your story ideas just before, or during, a slow news cycle in your community or business environment. Keep track of upcoming news events and work around them. For instance, if a State Senator is coming to town to announce new environmental funding, it may not be the best day to contact the local reporters and pitch your story idea—unless it ties in with the environmental theme.

Weeks following a holiday or other big event are often slow news weeks. Weekends are typically a quiet time in newsrooms. But be careful if you are dealing with small community news outlets—they may not have available staff on the weekends and you could end up with no coverage at all.

For journalists, determining whether a story is newsworthy could be based on how many stories they have that day to fill the pages or airtime. Your fundraiser may not get much coverage on the day the State Senator flies into town, but on a day when the reporters are looking for something newsworthy to report, it could land good coverage.

Tip: If you are dealing with community newspapers, keep an updated calendar of municipal meetings, school board meetings, and other community events. If the majority of public meetings fall during the second and fourth weeks of the month, send your releases during the first or third week.

Another timing issue is related to lengthy statements and news conferences. Nothing is dryer and more boring for a reporter than a press conference at which half-dozen speakers stand at a podium and read lengthy prepared statements. Lengthy prepared statements, long press releases (they should be one page) and drawn-out meetings bore many reporters, or muddy the issue, and could result is less coverage.

Never make a big announcement in the middle of a four-hour meeting. And unless you want to unveil a major news event or a big surprise announcement, lengthy press conferences are not an effective way to get good press coverage. A string of talking heads behind a podium does not make an interesting story and does not provide reporters with quality visuals and photos to accompany the news piece.

If you decide to announce something at a press conference, set up the podium or dais in front of a colorful backdrop or at an interesting location relative to the topic. Ask speakers to keep their comments brief. Bring charts or photos. Make a clever presentation rather than just offering dry speeches. Invite supporters or staff to serve as an audience so you have a presence aside from just the reporters. Do your research beforehand so that you schedule the press conference on a day when it won't compete with other news stories.

Visuals Make or Break a Story

As mentioned in an earlier chapter, visuals are key to getting better press coverage. Want your photo on the front page? Don't wear a white shirt and grey tie and expect to be in a photo on a front page printed in color.

Color print is used on the front page of many newspapers because it attracts the eye. The subject in the bright blue or red shirt may have a much better shot at landing on the front page than the one wearing black or grey.

Tip: Editors may choose an average story with great visuals over a great story with average visuals.

Television, print, and web news all need visuals to accompany their stories. A good photo or graphic can make the difference whether a story gets aired or published. Providing these images to reporters will help you get better coverage. When presiding over a meeting or making a presentation, liven things up—bring colorful signs, wear matching t-shirts or fill the room with graphics and photos. Get creative and add interest and action to an otherwise dry story.

There are times when a photograph *is* the entire story. You may be turned down for coverage after pitching an article idea, but the editor may agree to run a photo with a caption. Sometimes, they will send a staff photographer and on other occasions they will ask you to submit your own photos. Newspaper editors like photos that catch the eye and break up volumes of news text.

Never hesitate to submit photos of your charity event, business meeting, or campaign event to local papers, magazines, trade journals and community news web sites. They may not be chosen by an editor every time, but when they *are* published you get instant, free publicity.

Tip: Always offer to submit your own photos if the reporter shows up without a photographer or a camera.

News photos are unlike the standard pictures in your photo album. Editors typically don't want a photo of a group of people standing in a line and smiling. News photos should show action or emotion. The best photos show both.

Open a few newspapers and take a close look at the photos. A good news photo won't simply show a person standing at a podium speaking; the photo will show them raising their hand in a gesture, pointing to a map or chart, pushing their glasses up onto their nose. News photographers covering meetings will often hold the camera focused on one subject for long periods, waiting for the subject to gesture, point their fingers, scowl in disgust, show emotion. As soon as their subject displays some type of emotion or action, they take the shot.

People walking, a dog running in the background, someone laughing, cars speeding past the subject, one subject handing a document to another—these are all examples of movement within a photo. Don't show volunteers standing in a line at the food pantry posing for the shot—show them packing grocery bags or handing out food.

If assigned a story about an old theater slated for demolition, a good photographer won't just stand across the street and take a picture of the building. They will take the shot when pedestrians pass by or pause to read the demolition notice on the marquee.

Setting is also important in photos. Pictures of someone seated at their desk smiling at the camera are pretty boring. A photo of the same person at the same desk going over reports with staff is much more interesting.

For example, if you are submitting a photo of a Boy Scout car wash sponsored by your business, stage some scouts washing a sudsy car. Be certain to get some of the scout's faces in the photo and, if possible, set this entire scene up in front of a sign or banner displaying the name of your business or cause.

When taking your own photos to submit to a news editor, there are a few things to remember:

- Include some action or emotion whenever possible.

- Editors mostly work with high-resolution digital photos. Your pictures must be good quality and in sharp focus. Contact the editor and ask how they prefer photos be submitted.

- Zoom in. News photos have very little foreground. Your subject should be up close.

- Get creative. If you are taking a photo of your boss handling over a donation to the administrator of a local charity, stage the photo in a setting that suits the donation. Is it for a children's charity? Include some smiling kids. Save the beaches? Have your subjects seated on the dunes.

- If a photo must be taken in an office, stage the shot in front of a nice background— a bookcase or a flag. The subjects of the photo could shake hands while one presents the check to the other. At least there would be some minimal action.

- Be sure that the picture clearly shows the subject's faces.

Whenever possible, ask a reporter to interview you in person about a project or program. Describing the merits of a valuable program over the phone will have less of an impact and could result in minimal coverage. If a reporter witnesses the activities firsthand, they will likely give you more coverage. And if they don't bring a camera or a photographer, remember to provide your own photos.

Consider This: Visuals and Tangible Coverage

When I was reporting, a local non-profit pitched a story idea about a grief camp they held each summer for children who had lost a parent or close relative.

Editors passed on the story—the story was tricky. The newspaper could not identify the children so the story would be mainly a description of the camp. There was no clear-cut angle. Plus, it was a time-consuming assignment—the camp was 30 miles from the newsroom and in order to spend a day or two there, a reporter would have to pass on other stories.

But then a slow news week crept up about the same time the grief camp started. I took the assignment and spent two days at the camp, located on a breathtaking bluff off the coast of eastern Long Island. The story blossomed as I shadowed the campers, spoke to their parents, and interviewed the counselors. The article ended up a big success and the photos, carefully taken to protect the kid's identities, were compelling. Donations poured in to the non-profit.

Getting a reporter to witness your programs and events first-hand is a key to getting good press coverage. Always invite a reporter to visit so that they have a visual and can capture the emotion and tone of the story.

Teaming Up for Broader Coverage

If you are seeking coverage for an event, a program or your organization, there are several ways you can make your pitch more appealing to an editor or reporter.

Consider linking your idea into an event or holiday. Get a calendar of all the annual holidays—Flag Day, Veterans Day, Grandparents Day—there are dozens that have potential.

A New Jersey business held a pet parade on Flag Day. Pets and their owners showed up in red, white, and blue and the business owner handed out American flags. He marked out a parade route on his property, set up refreshment stands, and charged $1 for spectators. All the proceeds went to a local animal shelter. Several local newspapers and radio stations covered the parade.

Pairing up with a community activist or non-profit is a very effective way to obtain additional news coverage. If you have an idea you want to pitch to the local news, contact an activist in a related field and ask them to sit in on an interview, offer a quote in your press release, attend your press conference or speak at your event. By working together with a community activist, you will have more opportunities for coverage.

For example, when unveiling a computer program designed to provide public access to sex offender registration, one New York official invited administrators from every school district in the municipality, several community groups, law enforcement agents, the District Attorney and the director of a well-known regional children's advocacy group. The official listed all the invitees in a media advisory announcing the event. The lengthy list of attendees attracted reporters from a broad group of news outlets.

Be careful if you invite celebrities to support your cause. They can sometimes overshadow you and wrest attention away from the underlying message. (A journalist may choose to use the photo of the celebrity rather than the photo of you.) Instead, ask a celebrity or popular public official to write a letter to the editor in support of your cause. Or ask the celebrity to take a photo with you that *you* can submit for publication. When working with high-profile supporters, make sure the focus of the story remains on you and your cause.

Sponsoring local sports teams or scout programs is also a terrific way to get your name in the news. Offer to print banners, programs, and brochures for a Little League, charity, or community organization. Stay connected to your community by getting involved and simultaneously promote yourself.

If you want to bring additional attention to your cause or campaign, ask friends and supporters to write about it in blogs and in letters to the editor. Ask them to mention you or your situation to reporters they know. Get attention by word of mouth. Send promotional e-mails to everyone in your electronic address book and ask each person to send it to everyone in his or her e-mail address book. E-mails are a fast and free way to spread the word.

Consider This: Teaming Up:

A New York real estate office teamed up with a local charity that helps families in need obtain food, clothing and household supplies. The real estate agency "adopted" the charity and assigned an employee to serve as the liaison between the company and the non-profit.

The owners of the real estate company offered assistance on fundraising efforts and matched contributions made by their employees. An announcement of the partnership gained prominent press coverage in local newspapers.

This is a great example of how a business owner can become involved in the community, have a positive influence, and get press coverage.

Media Relations in the Digital Age

Connecting with the media once meant making phone calls and faxing press releases. But times have changed and today's digital world requires more of a news source. Using technology to spread the word is essential. Don't be intimidated by blogs and podcasts, they are actually quite simple to set up and they can reach large groups of supporters, clients, constituents and reporters quickly and inexpensively.

Faxed or e-mailed press releases, for the time being, remain a staple of media relations. But there is much more you can, and should, do to bring your message to the media and the public. If you are unfamiliar with new technology, these ideas can initially sound intimidating—but they are, in fact, quite easy to implement.

Here is a list of just a few of the ways you can bring attention to your business, cause or campaign:

Web site: Creating a web site for your business or cause can attract attention from both the media and the public. There are programs online (or on a MAC computer) that can help you develop you own web site—but in most cases it is advisable to hire a professional to design one for you.

A website reflects your image and provides all the pertinent details about you, your company, or your cause. Your web site should contain a press page with releases, photos and background information. Direct all reporters to your web site and update it regularly.

Never pass on an interview by telling a reporter that the information they need is on the site. Always choose a personal connection with a reporter over directing them to access the web site. The site can serve as an auxiliary source of information but should not replace you as a news source.

Blog: A blog, or web log, is a miniature web site used as an online diary or informational source. A blog is simple to set up and easy to manage.

Blogs have become a popular way to manage and distribute information. They can be used to update events or calendars, provide instant information, history, details, opinions, or photographs. Some blogs allow readers to leave comments and feedback.

Blogs are an effective way to post detailed information about a project or cause and to keep supporters updated. In many cases, you can augment news coverage by including information in your blog that the reporters did not include in their story.

To start a blog, take a look at online resources. There are blog services that allow you to start your own site for a small fee or even for free. If you have a MAC computer, you can start one through its iWEB function. Most blog building template sites are user-friendly and simple to manage. (Research the free sites carefully, some add advertisements to your pages.)

Your blog should include information about you, your contact information if you want feedback, and regularly updated entries. You can post press releases, transcripts, podcasts, photographs and anything else that will advance your press coverage. The blog entries can be archived so that viewers can read all your previous posts.

Announce your blog to all reporters who cover you and your cause and to any person or organization that may have an interest in your comments. For instance, if you are announcing an environmental initiative, send the blog to environmental advocacy groups and community organizations. If you are announcing a police union's safety program, send your blog to every public official and law enforcement agency in your county or state. Get people talking about your blog.

Podcast: A podcast is an audio or video broadcast, which can be played back on computers or media players, and some telephones. Podcasts are effective for promoting speeches, presentations, and even sermons. To start, you will need some simple recording equipment. A salesperson at any electronics store can show you exactly what you need. Then you can download software and start preparing, editing, and publishing your podcast.

With a podcast, officials and administrators can post speeches and interviews, business owners can show off a new product, and non-profits can illustrate the benefits of their outreach programs.

Prepare the content for your podcast and decide how long you want it to be. Again, I suggest brevity is the best option. Go online and research publishing options for your podcast (some sites are free, others may cost you a fee), upload the files and then announce your podcast on your blog and through mass e-mails.

Google Alert: Google offers an alert system that will automatically send you an e-mail update of the latest relevant Google results for whatever topic you select. Alerts are an easy way to monitor developing stories, keep updated on issues or people, keep tabs on a competitor, or monitor Internet postings about yourself.

Radio talk show: Local radio stations are a good way to get your message across. Many radio stations allocate time slots for interviews and talk segments. Contact the producer at stations and discuss the possibilities for a weekly or monthly radio show.

The same basic rules apply to electronic media relations as to interviews with reporters—stay focused and on-point. Don't talk too much or provide too many unnecessary details. Be truthful and drop all hyperbole. Be succinct.

Publicity Pyramid

When seeking press coverage, consider the pyramid theory again. This time, though, picture it right-side-up.

Local reporters, community news, and trade journals are a good way to kick off a publicity campaign for your story. Start small and then expand. Stories in a community newspaper or aired on a small television station are often picked up by larger news outlets. Large circulation newspapers and network television news broadcasts often get story ideas from small newspapers, web news sites, radio stations and small televisions stations. Staff at large news outlets research media reports from small communities where local reporters keep a closer eye on details.

Tip: Don't underestimate the power of the small press. If you successfully get coverage in a local newspaper, a larger news outlet could pick up the story later.

If possible, tie your story into a broader issue when pitching to the larger news outlet. For instance, a national charitable drive, the Super Bowl or popular sporting event, a widespread environmental concern, or a growing trend. There are endless ways you can generate local coverage by tying an event or cause into a larger issue that is getting broad national media coverage.

Also, keep in mind that reporters often begin their careers at community news outlets. By establishing a relationship with a local reporter, you could have a connection at a larger news outlet someday.

After a story is covered in a community newspaper or trade journal, submit the story to relative web sites, and put it on your own web site or blog.

Now, this doesn't mean that you shouldn't *try* to initially get coverage in the larger outlets. By all means pitch your story to daily newspapers, magazines, and network news. If the story is compelling enough you might beat the odds and get coverage. *But don't underestimate the power of the small press as a starting point.*

And never pass over your local reporters when pitching to a larger news outlet. If you deal with a regular group of reporters, pitch the story to them at the same time you present it to the large-scale media. If a local reporter feels snubbed by you, passed over for a more notable journalist, you may find yourself ignored on future stories. There is nothing worse for a reporter than learning about news from a rival reporter's story. Don't intentionally put your regular reporters in the position of being scooped by another reporter.

The Outshine Story

Stock up on a few newsworthy ideas that are timeless and that cast a positive reflection on you, your cause, your business, or your campaign. Keep these at bay until you need them. They can be unveiled at an opportune time to combat an unflattering story.

For example, the president of a law enforcement union is aware that his members manage an outreach program on their own time. They raise money to supply community children with car seats, bike helmets and sports equipment. Other members coach baseball and basketball teams in underprivileged neighborhoods. These are laudable programs and newsworthy community stories. Pitching these stories at the right time can help counteract unrelated negative coverage.

If an unflattering story is running in the local news about one of the union members, the president could pitch the outshine stories. He could invite reporters to play in the basketball games or challenge staff at a local newspaper to a game of softball—reporters versus volunteer coaches. Every player pitches in $10 and the money raised is donated to a local charity. Or he could ask a news photographer to join members when they deliver bike helmets to some needy children. There are countless ways to negate coverage by pitching an outshine story.

This will not work if you attempt to *create* news to serve as an outshine story. Outshine stories won't erase the negative coverage but they can provide some positive news to enhance your image and to combat bad press.

Crisis Information Management

The best advice for dealing with the media during a crisis is to be prepared in advance. Turmoil happens fast and there will typically be precious little time to prepare before reporters begin calling you.

Before an emergency situation arises, prepare a detailed plan of action. Appoint an emergency preparedness committee and assign specific tasks to each member. Committee members should each have their own responsibility for obtaining and sharing relevant information. A single media spokesperson should be appointed and all information should go through that person.

Tip: Obtain legal advice while preparing a plan of action for a crisis. An attorney may pick up on nuances in the plan that could present problems down the road.

First, decide exactly where the committee will meet in the event of a crisis situation. Provide folders to every member with contact information and background data relative to all potential emergency situations ranging from a natural disaster to an economic crisis to a colleague who has misstepped, resulting in damaging publicity.

One committee member should be appointed as the liaison to bosses, elected officials, supervisors, or stakeholders. Another should have a press release template ready so they can quickly fill in the blanks and send out releases. Several members should be appointed to handle incoming messages and inquiries. At least one person should be charged with coordinating the activities of the other committee members and keeping records of the progress.

Once a crisis unfolds, establish a schedule for doling out information to the public. Schedule an initial press conference (or prepare a press release) and include background and all pertinent information. Then set regular updates. If the event is timely and impacting a large group of people (a storm, crime wave, or wildfire) the updates should be scheduled every few hours. A corporate meltdown that transpires slowly should have weekly updates.

Post updates about the crisis resolution plan on your blog and web site. Send public service announcements to local radio stations. Cover every base to get the information out to the media and to the public. Try to arrange *live* televised interviews so that your *exact* comments are aired.

In advance of a real emergency, committee members should 'practice" interviewing the appointed spokesperson by asking questions related to any number of potential calamities. Go over all possible scenarios and anticipated questions and hold mock interviews. This is an effective tactic—one, by the way, used by the White House—and the exercise could prevent confusing responses and unintentional slip-ups when the real deal is underway.

If the crisis is a natural disaster or an emergency that requires providing swift and comprehensive information to the public, choose a reporter you trust and ask them to shadow you or a staff member. If there is no risk of leaking confidential information or compromising public safety, this is an effective way to demonstrate that you are actively assisting with the flow of information. (Check with an attorney and law enforcement or other public safety officials before inviting a reporter along.) And although I advise against playing favorites, this is a situation where you should choose just one reporter. In most crisis situations, a gaggle of journalists following you around could be distracting and problematic.

When pitching news stories to reporters or editors:

Don'ts:

- Don't send mass e-mails to anonymous recipients. Address each one individually.

- Don't demand to be covered.

- Don't exaggerate in hopes of gaining their interest.

- Don't underestimate the power of the small press.

- Don't send lengthy documents as your pitch.

- Don't announce big news during long meetings.

Do's:

- Do submit your own photos.

- Do keep your pitch brief and interesting.

- Do pitch the story well in advance of deadline.

- Do tie your story idea into a larger issue or theme.

- Do team up with an activist and community groups.

- Do use blogs, podcasts and web sites as promotional tools.

Step Eight:
Press Release Clinic

Press releases and press conferences still have their place, albeit diminished, in the world of media relations. If presented correctly, they remain effective ways to get press coverage. Press releases should announce a general topic or event and should be faxed and e-mailed to all reporters simultaneously and posted on your web site or blog.

Never "embargo" press releases. Embargoes, a demand that the information in the release not be publicized until a specified time or date, were commonly used prior to the introduction of fax machines and computers. In those days, announcements were generally made by phone or by regular mail. The intention of an embargo was to give all the reporters an equal amount of time to release the news. These days, you can inform journalists simultaneously and there are very few instances where an embargo is warranted.

Press releases are generally preferred over press conferences unless the news is really momentous and there are numerous new sources connected to the announcement. Press conferences allow all the reporters and all the sources to get together and discuss the news as a group. Reserve press conferences for the really significant news events. They are time-consuming for reporters. (And most journalists particularly despise when a parade of verbose speakers take turns at the microphone crowing about their own accomplishments.)

Tip: Keep speeches under 20 minutes and press releases to one page.

If the topic allows, get creative and invite reporters to an alternative type of press conference. For instance, officials looking to announce the results of a comprehensive beach erosion prevention plan could hold a press conference in a meeting room where they announce the results, show aerial photos and provide data. *Or* they could invite reporters and residents to walk the beach with them, showing them the bolstered dunes and providing relevant information along the way. The latter option could attract more reporters and ultimately land broader coverage.

If you do decide to hold a press conference, send a media advisory announcing the time and place of the event. Try to give reporters 24 hours notice at the very least. Do not reveal all the information about the news story in the media advisory or there will be no reason for the reporters to show up.

Tip: Media advisories about a press conference should just include the general topic, where and when the event will be held, and the names of the participants. If you include all the information to be announced at the press conference, reporters may not show up.

Bring bullet points (in bold type and large font) for speaking at a press conference—do not read long written statements. Look up at the attendees, not down at your paperwork. Keep the conference to less than 30 minutes. Distribute folders with back-up statistics and data, the names and titles of all participants, contact numbers and e-mails, and any other relevant information.

Different Releases for Different Types of Stories

There are different ways to prepare releases depending on the nuances of the related story. For a quick, brief announcement that requires little or no follow-up (the rescheduling of a meeting for example) a short media advisory is enough.

For a story that you *want* your name attached to—and if you hope the reporters will call you for additional comment—prepare the release but omit a quote. Submit the release well in advance of deadline to give reporters ample time to contact you for comment.

If you really want to stack the odds in your favor that a reporter will contact you directly for additional information about a news release, omit a pertinent piece of information. If you leave out an essential element, reporters must contact you to fill in the gaps. This will give you the opportunity to embellish on the information or to bring up a relative story that you want to discuss in tandem with the news presented in the press release.

On the flip side, if you are compelled to send a press release but are not pleased about the news being delivered, you may want to distance yourself. In this case, include all the details about the issue, anticipate every question a reporter may have and provide all the pertinent information (Who, What, Where, When, and Why). Provide enough detail to allow them to prepare their entire story from the release. Include at least one quote. You will fulfill an obligation to provide the news but you may stave off a barrage of unwanted questions—at least temporarily. At this point, it could be time to unveil the "outshine story" in advance of the next news cycle. (See previous chapter for description of an outshine story.)

When seeking publicity for an event that has already passed, it is unlikely that a television news station will have too much interest. When sending a release to the print news or to web news about an event that has already occurred, attach photos for a better chance of getting coverage and make sure the announcement is newsworthy and not simply promotional.

Consider This: Press Releases

A press release from the office of a small-town elected official announced that he had recently spent an afternoon visiting students at one of the schools in his district. As you might expect, this release garnered no press coverage.

There are myriad problems with this type of release. First, the event had already occurred. The release should have been sent *prior* to the visit so that reporters could have had the opportunity to attend, perhaps shadow the official as he met with the students. (But even then, a random visit to a school is not very newsworthy.)

The next problem was that the official was promoting himself— and not very effectively, He forgot to consider if there was any conflict, change, or color within the story he was pitching. He was not visiting the school because of an unusual event or special program; he was not there to announce additional funding; he was not presenting the students with an award. He was simply visiting the students. His visit was just not newsworthy.

Sources must entice the media with a press release. Some editors might receive hundreds of releases every week. A good press release stands out. Tips from Step One (positioning yourself within the story) can help you to craft a press release that will attract press coverage. Don't forget that the 3 C's (conflict, change and color) must be part of your news pitch.

Media Kits

Media kits are generally only effective if you are concentrating on an issue that reporters will *absolutely* want to cover. A media kit promoting your existing business with nothing new or newsworthy included is a waste of time and money. However, if you want to spread the word about an ambitious new project that will impact a large group of people or if you are kicking off a campaign, then media kits can generate positive press coverage.

A media kit is basically an enhanced press release. It should have single focus and include comprehensive information. Assemble the information for the media kit in a folder or a single electronic file.

Media kits typically include a press release or cover letter (sometimes both) announcing the news plus contact information, photos, graphs, charts and reports, background information, and profiles.

Consider this example: a Maryland-based environmental advocacy group is launching a new fundraising effort aimed at protecting wetlands along the entire Eastern Seaboard. The group would like to announce the initiative to hundreds of news outlets from Maine to Florida. Since most of these journalists are not familiar with the group or its extensive advocacy history, a media kit will allow them to provide reporters with the background on the group and information on their new initiative.

(This phantom environmental group, to avoid criticism over wasteful use of paper, would be best advised to send electronic media kits.)

The kit should include:

- An overview of the proposed project.
- A contact information sheet that includes numbers and emails for the group's staff plus any elected officials who support the effort.
- Background on the group and several news articles about their past advocacy efforts.
- Celebrity endorsements.
- Charts and graphs with statistics on the sensitive wetlands and the cost of the proposed protection efforts.

Each media kit should be addressed to an editor or reporter at each individual news outlet. Ideally, a short introduction with information about specific wetlands regions within each new outlet's coverage area should be included.

Media kits can be expensive and time-consuming so only use them if the news you are pitching is truly significant and newsworthy. Apply the *so what?* test and ask yourself whether the issue is one that will be of interest to the media and to the public.

How to Write a Press Release

An effective press release must be written in a very specific way. The news must be presented in a concise manner and the release must answer some basic questions. In most instances, press releases should be kept to one page.

When I was reporting for a weekly newspaper, one official frequently sent lengthy press releases with far more information than we cared to read. When these five page, single-spaced, releases were taken off the fax machine, standard practice by the entire editorial staff was to take the first and last page and toss the rest. We would get the gist of the story and call sources for fresh quotes and background.

One page is more than enough in most cases to incorporate the essential information. A press release announces a story, and then a journalist will do the rest. The exception to the one-page rule is when photographs, charts, diagrams or reports accompany the release.

Remember, the goal is to be informative. A press release is not a resume or a report.

Before writing a release, remember the inverted pyramid rule. News stories are prepared under this premise with the most vital information at the beginning and then narrowing in importance as the story proceeds. Your press release should be constructed precisely the same way.

The press release should provide basic answers to the 5W's. *Who? What? When? Where?* and *Why.* Sometimes a *How* gets tossed into the equation.

There are some variations, but typically a standard release is single-spaced with double spaces between paragraphs. The tone should be professional and non-emotional, written just as any straight news article would be written.

In the upper left corner—or right if you prefer—write 'press release' in capital, bold letters. Directly underneath, put the date and underneath that put a contact name, with their exact title, along with a phone number and email address. (A template for press releases follows later in this chapter.)

Headline: Next, write a concise headline announcing the main news. You may want to add a subheadline in slightly smaller font elaborating on the news. Both these headlines should be centered above the body of the text of the release. They do not need periods at the end. (And never put an exclamation point.) Sometime the headline is all in caps: in other instances only the first letter of major words are capitalized (not *the* or *and* or *a*). However, there is no steadfast rule—this is a simply a stylistic preference.

The headline and subheadline should be written in the present tense, even if describing past events. For example, if your department won a noteworthy award for financial accounting then create a catchy headline with some interesting elements to spice up what could otherwise be a dry topic.

Do not write:

Headline: *City Finance Office Received Accounting Award*
Subhead: *This is the 3rd Year In a Row the Office Won This Award*

Instead, keep the headline in the present tense and the words concise. Try this:

Headline: *City Finance Office Wins Prestigious National Award*
Subhead: *Mayor Hails City Staff For Stellar Accounting Practices*

The second example grabs the reader's attention. There are two components—the announcement of the award plus the mayor's favorable reaction. It is fresh, presents more information, sells the story and it uses active words.

The first example is dry. The subheadline in the first example includes old news. It is indeed interesting that the city won the award three consecutive years but that detail belongs in the body of the press release.

Body of the release: The body of the release should be written in short, declarative sentences. The body is often written in the past tense and should be four or five paragraphs.

First paragraph: The first paragraph should indicate who you are and exactly what you are announcing. "Springfield Mayor Joe Smith announced on October 1 that the city finance office has won a prestigious national accounting award from the Governor's office…….." If the event has past, add when and where the department received the award. If the award has yet to be presented, include the date and location of the awards ceremony and who is expected to attend.

If you are sending the release outside your own community, start the first paragraph with a tag line for *your* city or town. For instance, begin the first paragraph with an italicized *San Francisco* followed by a dash. Then begin your first sentence. This is not necessary if the release is only being sent to the greater San Francisco area.

Second paragraph: The second paragraph should state why the news is important. Perhaps the award will secure a better financial rating for the city, resulting in lower taxes. Here may be the appropriate place to note that this is the third consecutive year that this particular office has received the award.

Third and fourth paragraphs: The third and fourth paragraphs should include background and, if appropriate, a quote. Quotes should be one or two sentences with "said Mayor Joe Smith." at the end of the quote. Always include the title and full name of whoever is being quoted and use the word *said*. Avoid using *stated* or *gasped* or *promised* to connect the quote to the speaker. Just use *said*. (and never use *says*—use the past tense for quotes.)

Final paragraph: The final paragraph should include a one-sentence description of the company or department. Then repeat the contact person and information from the top of the page. This paragraph can also include references to web sites, books, or other resources that would provide additional details.

End release: Underneath the last sentence, center three asterisks *** to indicate the end of the release.

Always ask a colleague to review the release before you send it out. Self-editing is difficult and a fresh pair of eyes will cull out many errors and omissions. If appropriate, run it by your supervisor or the company's attorneys. Never send a press release on behalf of a company or department without clearing it through the proper channels. Remember, once they are out there, you can't take them back.

Tip: Check out the official website for your State Governor's or State Senator's office and review the online press releases. Read several and you will get a handle on the tone of how standard releases are written.

Be sure to put the release on letterhead or include a logo so that it is clear to reporters precisely who sent the press release. If the topic is an ongoing issue and this particular release is an update, attach previous releases you sent on the same topic. Make sure each of the press releases is dated.

If you send out several press releases per week, individually number each release. Start the new year with a new number—for example, begin in 2009 with the first release of the year number 1-2009; followed by 2-2009 and so on. Place the number at the very bottom of the page or underneath the contact line in the upper corner.

Send your press releases by fax and e-mail to any reporters and organizations you suspect would have an interest in the subject. Post the release on your web site and blog. Send one to local radio stations. In some cases, radio announcers will read portions of the release verbatim during news reports.

(*Template for a Press Release*)

PRESS RELEASE
Date:
Contact: Mr. News Source, title, telephone number. E-mail address

Headline Announces the News in the Present Tense, Bolded, and Larger Font Than the Body of the Release.

Subhead Should be Bolded, Centered, Smaller Font Than the Headline, Present Tense, and Should Embellish Main Theme

First paragraph: single spaced in 11 or 12-point font. This paragraph should indicate who is announcing the news and provide the answers to *when?* and *where?*

Second paragraph: explains why the news is important, whom it impacts, and how it came about.

Third paragraph: one or two sentence quote from the person announcing the news or other appropriate news source. "The quote should be succinct and support the headline and the theme in the second paragraph," said Mr. News Source. "An opinion or praise is often suitable here."

Fourth paragraph: background on the issue and any relevant statistics can be included here. If supporting information is lengthy, attach documentation to the release.

Final paragraph: Any boilerplate information on the person or company making the announcement (e.g. Mr. News Source has been the elected president for ten years. The company headquarters is located in New York City.) If you have space left on the page, repeat the contact information. *For additional information, contact…..*

***

(*Template for a Media Advisory*)

MEDIA ADVISORY
Date: one to two days prior to the press conference or event.
Contact: Mr. News Source, title, telephone number, E-mail address

Media Advisory:

Springfield—Mr. News Source, title, and his staff will host a press conference on (date) at (time) at (location) to announce results of the city's teen recreation survey.

Invited speakers include Springfield City Mayor Joe Smith, Springfield Recreation Superintendent Mary Jones, School Superintendent Bob West, members of the City Council, and local high school students who assisted with the survey.

The recreation survey was authorized at a meeting of the City Council on May 2, 2007. Additional information will be distributed at the event.

***

Journalism Jargon

If you deal with reporters regularly, it's important to understand some of the language commonly used in most newsrooms. Here is just a sampling of terms you may hear when dealing with reporters:

Attribution: Linking the information to a specific source. Naming the source; attributing the comments or details to someone within the story.

Not for Attribution: An agreement between reporter and source that the information will not be linked, or attributed, to them when it is used in a news story.

Beat: A specific area that a reporter covers. A beat can be tangible (a city, a political campaign, a school district) or intangible (the arts, sports, business).

Byline: The name, and sometimes title, of the author of a newspaper or magazine article. (*By Joe Smith*) which typically appears between the headline and the first paragraph or at the bottom of the article.

Clarification vs. Correction: A news outlet may offer to run a clarification if a source complains that a truncated quote changed the meaning of the comments or if another type of misunderstanding clouded the coverage. They are not admitting an error—they are clarifying the nuances of a story. A correction is a statement from the editor or publisher correcting erroneous facts reported in a previous news story.

Copy: The actual text of a news story.

Deadline: The exact time that the reporter must submit their final story to an editor or producer.

Editorial: Opinion piece prepared by editors, publishers and producers.

Editorial Board: A group of editors, publishers, and journalists who make up the official leadership of a news outlet. The editorial board makes decisions about the position of a news outlet, what stories will run, and the tone of the content.

Embargo: Request by a source that information be held confidential for a pre-set amount of time before the reporter delivers the news.

Exclusive: A story that just a single news outlet has access to.

Feature story: A news piece that is an overview of a person, place, or situation. Features are not breaking news events but tend to be more entertaining.

Graph: Slang for "paragraph"

Hook: The most interesting element of the story and the reason why the story makes the news.

Lede: The opening or first paragraph in a news story. (some journalists use 'lead')

Live mike: A microphone that is on, picking up, recording or transmitting sound.

Media Advisory: A brief release sent to the media announcing an upcoming event or issuing a statement. Advisories are much less detailed than press releases.

Off the record: An agreement between news source and reporter that all information discussed is confidential, not to be used in the story, and not to be linked to the source.

On background: Agreement between source and reporter that all information provided is for background purposes and not for attribution.

Paraphrase: When a reporter sums up a sources comments rather than quoting them verbatim.

Pitch: When a source suggests a story for coverage to a reporter, he "pitches" the idea.

Press Kit/Media Kit: A folder, package, or web link with promotional material on an organization, business, cause, or campaign.

PSA: Public Service Announcement. A free commercial or ad intended to inform the public about a crisis situation or to help a non-profit etc.

Pull quote: In print news, when a quote is highlighted within the text of an article. Sometimes referred to as "call outs" these quotes are enlarged, placed in text boxes, or italicized to draw attention to the comment and to break up long columns of copy.

Round-up story: A news piece on a broad topic that highlights a variety of quotes or examples. For instance, a round up on unique holiday shopping opportunities will include a brief introduction and then a long list of retail shops and special items they offer.

Scooped: When a journalist is beat out on a story by a rival reporter.

Sidebar: A short story that accompanies and embellishes a larger story. For example, a news story on Northern California might include a sidebar on popular vineyards.

Spin: Version of a story that is presented in a slanted way as a means of benefitting a source, campaign, company, or organization.

Subhead: A second headline in a news story or press release that expands on the main headline.

Lightning Source UK Ltd.
Milton Keynes UK
UKOW051222020512

191869UK00001B/22/P